CW01378995

HOW LEADERS LEARN TO BOOST CREATIVITY IN TEAMS

Innovation Catalysts

Other Related Titles from World Scientific

Creativity, Imagination and Innovation: Perspectives and Inspirational Stories
edited by Xavier Pavie
ISBN: 978-981-3272-99-6

Innovation and Entrepreneurship: Choice and Challenge
by Otto Chui Chau Lin
ISBN: 978-981-3146-60-0

Innovation Heroes: Understanding Customers as a Valuable Innovation Resource
by Fiona Schweitzer and Joe Tidd
ISBN: 978-1-78634-536-3

The Scale-up Manual: Handbook for Innovators, Entrepreneurs, Teams and Firms
by Uday Phadke and Shailendra Vyakarnam
ISBN: 978-1-78634-590-5
ISBN: 978-1-78634-626-1 (pbk)

HOW LEADERS LEARN TO BOOST CREATIVITY IN TEAMS
Innovation Catalysts

Rob Sheffield

University of the West of England, UK

World Scientific

NEW JERSEY · LONDON · SINGAPORE · BEIJING · SHANGHAI · HONG KONG · TAIPEI · CHENNAI · TOKYO

Published by

World Scientific Publishing Europe Ltd.
57 Shelton Street, Covent Garden, London WC2H 9HE
Head office: 5 Toh Tuck Link, Singapore 596224
USA office: 27 Warren Street, Suite 401-402, Hackensack, NJ 07601

Library of Congress Control Number: 2018029676

British Library Cataloguing-in-Publication Data
A catalogue record for this book is available from the British Library.

HOW LEADERS LEARN TO BOOST CREATIVITY IN TEAMS
Innovation Catalysts

Copyright © 2019 by World Scientific Publishing Europe Ltd.

All rights reserved. This book, or parts thereof, may not be reproduced in any form or by any means, electronic or mechanical, including photocopying, recording or any information storage and retrieval system now known or to be invented, without written permission from the Publisher.

For photocopying of material in this volume, please pay a copying fee through the Copyright Clearance Center, Inc., 222 Rosewood Drive, Danvers, MA 01923, USA. In this case permission to photocopy is not required from the publisher.

ISBN 978-1-78634-620-9

For any available supplementary material, please visit
https://www.worldscientific.com/worldscibooks/10.1142/Q0185#t=suppl

Desk Editors: Dipasri Sardar/Jennifer Brough/Koe Shi Ying

Typeset by Stallion Press
Email: enquiries@stallionpress.com

To Rachael, for everything

About the Author

Rob Sheffield is a coach, consultant and trainer, specialising in helping leaders enable creativity and innovation in their organisations. He holds a PhD (Organisation Studies) from the University of the West of England, where he is also a Visiting Fellow.

He writes, researches, teaches and has consulted with organisations including EY, GE Healthcare, Mercer and the UK National Health System. His current research is focusing on the Leadership of Innovation in Health and Social Care.

He presents at networks and conferences throughout Europe and UK. Recently, he presented at the *International Society for Professional Innovation Management* (ISPIM) in Porto and the *Developing Leadership Capability Conference* (DLCC) in Bristol. He co-wrote a chapter, with Prof. Carol Jarvis and Jane Hadfield, which was shortlisted and included in the *Paris Innovation & Entrepreneurship Teaching Excellence Awards 2017*.

Rob believes that creativity is being learnt and applied, judiciously, in many organisational contexts.

(Unfortunately, he's not the much more famous 'Rob Sheffield', who works for Rolling Stone magazine in New York.) Instead, this author can be reached via www.bluegreenlearning.com or at rob@bluegreenlearning.com.

Acknowledgements

I want to thank the various people who helped with this book.

First, thanks to the people who contributed cases, stories or interviews for the book, including Professor Carol Jarvis, Jonathan Hammond-Williams, Shelley Harris, Donna Biggs, Charlie Widdows, Professor Carlo Ratti, Wendy Fowles-Sweet, Lisa Brodie, Farzad Eskafi, Rob Jackson and Dr Karen Blakeley.

I'm grateful to the many clients whose fascinating work challenges gave opportunities for the ideas in this book to emerge. There's little as rewarding as working with good people on worthwhile, tricky problems. Thanks to the people at EY, Mercer, GE Healthcare, Burnham Rosen, Solverboard and University of the West of England and to the people across organisations in the UK National Health System. I am thankful to Christina Quinn and her team at the NHS South West Leadership Academy.

Thanks to those smart, committed work friends whose inspiration, support and conversations over many years have enriched the ideas in this book — in particular, Jane James, Carol Jarvis, Jane Hadfield, Peter Simpson, Martin Codrington, David Leigh and Anne Stenbom.

I was inspired by outstanding work carried out across decades by very many people. In the leadership and power field, too much has been forgotten about the extraordinary 'motives' work led by David McClelland and his team of researchers, including David Burnham. In the area of creativity, I could not have written this book without the research, teaching and applied practice of Goran Ekvall and Scott Isaksen on the climate for innovation, Michael Kirton's adaption-innovation theory, the many scholars from Buffalo State University who systematised an approach to creative problem solving and the initial work of Mel Rhodes.

Authority figures leave a mark. My approach to learning was changed forever by an excellent geography teacher when I was 17. His name is Peter Rowbotham. My second manager, Katy Weston, is an excellent coach, and helped me learn plenty, quickly.

Thanks to my editor, Jennifer Brough, who was patient, generous with her time and support, and unwaveringly positive.

Also, thanks to my wife, Rachael, for the practical and emotional help you gave. I couldn't have written this without you. And, Ella and Cormac, thanks for making me stop thinking of this book.

Contents

About the Author vii
Acknowledgements ix
List of Figures xv
List of Tables xvii

How Leaders Learn to Boost Creativity in Teams:
Innovation Catalysts 1

Chapter 1 The Creativity Convergence — A Meeting of Need,
Means and Want 3
Relevance for the Reader 5
The Topicality of Creativity and Innovation 6
The Demand for Innovation is Growing 7
Delivering Innovation is Proving to be Difficult 12
Innovation and Reification 14
The Innovation Bind 15
A *Cri de Coeur* for the Age of Creativity 20
References 23

Chapter 2 Rethinking Power and Leadership 27
Research Overview: Power and Leadership 28
Training in the Power Motive 36
The Power Motive and Leadership 38

	The Leadership of Creativity and Innovation	45
	References	48
Chapter 3	Aligning Everyday Innovation with Strategy	49
	Research Overview: Creativity and Purposeful Outcomes	51
	Organisations are Changing from the Outside-in and Inside-out	57
	References	58
Chapter 4	Building the Skills for Creativity	61
	Research Overview: The Development of Creative Problem Solving	63
	Divergent and Convergent Thinking	68
	Principles for Divergent Thinking	72
	Story: The Hagrid Concept	74
	Principles for Convergent Thinking	75
	Components of the Creative Problem-Solving Model	77
	Component 1: Understanding the Challenge	78
	Component 2: Generating Ideas	82
	Component 3: Preparing for Implementation	87
	Ten Practical Implications for Leaders	89
	Case 1: The Ambulance Service	91
	Case 2: The Drug and Alcohol Dependency Team	93
	Case 3: The Creative-writing Workshop	96
	Chapter Review: Key Learning from Building CPS Skills	99
	References	101
Chapter 5	Work Context — A Healthy Climate for Innovation	103
	Research Overview: How Climate Affects Innovation Performance	105
	Leadership, Climate and Goodwill	108
	Climate and the Situational Outlook Questionnaire	110
	The SOQ Climate Tool	114
	Case 1: Solverboard — The Open Innovation People	114

		Case Review	118
		Case 2: The Healthcare Unit	119
		Chapter Review — Key Learning on Creating a Healthy Climate	128
		References	129
Chapter 6		Making Use of Different Perspectives	133
		Research Overview: The Role of Adaption-innovation Theory in Creative Problem Solving	134
		Story: Experimenting with the KAI	140
		The Leader and the Problem-solving Process	141
		Research Support for Adaption-innovation Theory	142
		Summarising Adaption-innovation Differences	144
		So What? Reflections on Adaption-innovation Theory	147
		Story: Unsuccessful Leader Coping	151
		Story: A Fishy Tale…	155
		Case 1: The Law Firm — More Structure Please	156
		Case Review	158
		Case 2: An Effective Pairing	158
		Case Review	162
		Case 3: Fitting People to the Work	164
		Case Review	168
		Chapter Review — Practical Learning on Optimising Cognitive Diversity	169
		References	171
Chapter 7		Sustaining Creativity Across Time and Scale	173
		Case 1: The Radical Education Offering	174
		Case Review	183
		Book Synthesis and Limitations	185
		Potential Scenarios: Wider Creativity in Society	186
		References	189

Further Resources   191

Index   193

List of Figures

Figure 1.1:	Incorporating novelty	16
Figure 2.1:	The ABCD model	47
Figure 3.1:	ABCD model — Align innovation efforts to strategic goals	50
Figure 4.1:	ABCD model — Build creative problem-solving skills	62
Figure 4.2:	Creative problem-solving process	66
Figure 5.1:	ABCD model — Create the work climate for idea development	105
Figure 5.2:	Solverboard team SOQ results	115
Figure 6.1:	ABCD model — Leverage the diversity of your people	134
Figure 6.2:	Results distribution for KAI profiles	137
Figure 6.3:	Estimating KAI preference	147

List of Tables

Table 2.1:	Source and target of power	34
Table 4.1:	Creative problem-solving components overview	77
Table 4.2:	Creative problem-solving tools and their 'fit' for incremental and radical change	85
Table 5.1:	Podiatry leadership team initial climate results	119
Table 5.2:	Podiatry leadership team repeat climate results	124
Table 5.3:	Diabetic implementation team, initial and repeat climate results	126
Table 6.1:	Adaption–innovation characteristic differences	145
Table 6.2:	Adaption–innovation coping strategies	150
Table 6.3:	Ebusiness team KAI results	157
Table 6.4:	SME business team KAI results	165

How Leaders Learn to Boost Creativity in Teams: Innovation Catalysts

Chapter 1

The Creativity Convergence — A Meeting of Need, Means and Want

> We have to continually be jumping off cliffs and developing our wings on the way down.
>
> **Ray Bradbury**

This is an optimistic book, arguing that leaders are playing a key role, in bringing diverse people together, to develop novel solutions that fit the needs of the people they serve, and make those people's lives better. Many are doing this, through their focus, determination, skills and collaboration with others, and in ways that rarely make headlines. Mostly, these leaders are not interested in making headlines, but they're doing the work anyway. And this is timely, because, as we'll see, the need for, means of and motivation for creativity are converging.

The ideas in this book have evolved at the boundary of organisational research and practice in working with leaders and teams. The work has covered 30 years, and spanned the UK, Continental Europe, USA, China and India, working with global companies and smaller, vibrant ones across healthcare, professional and legal services, education and technology. It's been a fascinating and fortunate time to be involved in this work, because the paradigm of leadership has altered, away from the taken-for-granted focus on the leader as a heroic individual, to one of leadership as a more distributed and relational process.

My colleagues and I work with many leaders who are learning and applying lessons in their teams, organisations and collaborating beyond their organisational boundaries. Part of the motivation for writing this book is fuelled by the dissonance experienced between our everyday work with leaders, and the news-grabbing headlines around leadership:

> We now observe a huge divide between the modest trust in institutions of business and government and a pitifully low level of confidence in their leaders. Over two-thirds of the general population do not have confidence that current leaders can address their country's challenges. The credibility of CEOs fell by 12 points this year to 37 percent globally; in Japan, it is 18 percent.[1]

Much of this distrust is driven by an increasing sense that current systems of wealth creation and redistribution are perceived to be meeting the needs of only a small minority. At more local levels, corrupt leaders damage the reputation of their organisations, and leaders elsewhere, as officers of organisations, are tarred by association.

But there are also grounds for hope from this report. Around 75% of the survey respondents believed that business could both increase profits and improve the conditions in communities where it operates. And, of those unsure as to whether the system works for them, 58% trust business the most. Many people want business to do more social good.

We know how easy it is for leaders to stimulate cynicism, anger and suspicion. And, once freed, these genies are not easily contained. Hope, optimism and pride in results take longer to cultivate, but are present in the lives of many leaders who are currently doing good work. And we encounter many examples of leaders who work hard to serve their customers, clients, patients, service users and wider communities.

This book is an attempt to give those learning leaders a voice. I want to point out that much good work is being done by mature leaders, who are learning to use their power, to energise the people around them, making things better for the people they serve.

That's about the 'why'. As for the 'what', the focus of this book is on creativity as it feeds into a wider innovation process. I have tried to integrate previously separate strands of research and practice from the fields of creativity, innovation and leadership, into a coherent framework.

The emphasis is on informing leadership practice, illustrating principles through the real-life experiences of organisational leaders.

The intended audience is people in leadership roles, who are being challenged to develop innovative approaches to work, delivered through the teams they lead.

Some of the stories in the book are illustrations of work done well, and, sometimes, not so well. The cases in Chapters 4, 5, 6 and 7 come from interviews with people with whom my colleagues and I have worked in recent years. All of these people have delivered noteworthy change in their organisations. Other interviews through the book provide contextual examples of what's changing in this growing area of work. These people are engaged in developing substantial, often leading-edge, work, applying human and/or machine technologies which are often based on solid research. In total, I interviewed 15 people, 12 in recorded interviews and 3 by email. Some of their names and organisations' names are changed to meet their organisational policies on anonymity and confidentiality; some are shared in straightforward interview formats; some are retrospective accounts, co-written by me and verified with others; some are written-up interviewee accounts, responding to questions asked by me.

Relevance for the Reader

You will find the book useful and inspiring, if you

- are a leader, at frontline, middle or senior level, in business, the public sector, government or community organisations;
- are curious about how to develop ideas with your team, from first insights to proven concept;
- are studying creativity and innovation and want both an overview of research and practical examples of real people applying learning in their work;
- want to grow your own capacity for creativity and innovation, but don't know where to start. Have faith! There are well-tested ways to do this, developed through decades of research and practice;
- intuit that the importance of creativity and innovation is growing, but don't know why. You're right! Read on...

You'll also know that you can't deliver innovation by yourself. Other people probably have better ideas — there are more of them than you! The energetic commitment of your team to introducing new ways of working is crucial to seeing things through and delivering value. The work is simply too complex for any one person to solve.

You will know that your people demand a certain degree of challenge and want to keep learning, partly for the 'buzz', but also to safeguard their future employability. You feel responsible to help them with that.

Moreover, for yourself, you have a life outside of work, and you value it. Working 14-hour days does not appeal. Perhaps you belong to the so-called sandwich generation — looking after your children and your parent(s). Either way, work is vitally important but it's not everything.

Equally, your team needs you, in your leadership role. How you conceive your role, and think about using your power and authority, will have a clear and sustained impact on others' commitment and performance.

The Topicality of Creativity and Innovation

> Innovation is today's equivalent of the holy grail. Rich-world governments see it as a way of staving off stagnation. Poor governments see it as a way of speeding up growth. And business people everywhere see it as the key to survival.[2]

But as the terms *innovation* and *creativity* have become more commonplace, their meanings have become a little foggy. Exploring the academic literature, creativity is most commonly described as the generation of novel and useful ideas,[3] while innovation involves the successful implementation of creative ideas by the organisation, leading to value creation for stakeholders.[4]

In this view, creativity is an essential early stage of the innovation process. Our experience suggests that, in many organisations, creativity is not really trusted. It's the black sheep of innovation, which sounds more business-like, solid and incontestable. But, as Isaksen *et al.* put it:

> Our position is simple. You can have creativity without innovation, but you cannot have innovation without creativity.[5] (p. 14)

Thinking of creativity as a necessary sub-set of the more complex innovation process is useful. As a broad simplification, being able to conceptualise novel and useful ideas at an early stage is an essential precondition for innovation. And novelty needn't mean new to the whole world. The consensus is that new-in-context is novel enough. And think of 'useful' as having the potential to bring value to relevant stakeholders.

In this book, when I'm referring to the early stages of the development of novel and useful ideas, I'm talking about creativity; when we're referring to the whole process, or to value realisation through implementation and spread of ideas, I call it innovation.

At this point, let's review Rhodes' model which has had an enduring impact on the field of human creativity. In reviewing the creativity literature, Rhodes collected 56 definitions of creativity and synthesised them into 4 main themes of *Product, Process, Press and Person*.[6]

- *The creative product*: How creative is the outcome produced? Whether that is a product, service, process, business model, market and so on. And what are the qualities or attributes of creative outcomes that make them 'creative'?
- *The creative process*: This looks at *how* ideas develop, as well as the development of thinking tools, rules, tips and practices to nurture ideas through phases of development. This is where much training and consultancy work focuses, and with good reason, since this is most closely connected with explicit idea development.
- *The creative press*: Work context makes a difference. Sometimes, ably-skilled individuals and groups just don't apply their talents because of factors in the local environment.
- *The creative person*: What are the traits and styles of people that seem to influence the number, variety, originality and detail of their ideas?

Rhodes was interested in the integrative nature of his framework. He believed that these themes, in combination, could provide a useful governing structure for creativity that could be helpful for the deliberate and meaningful application of creativity in our everyday work.

The Demand for Innovation is Growing

However, it works and whatever we can learn about it, the demand for innovative solutions is growing, and several factors are driving the need. First, of course, organisations need ideas. Anyone working can barely spend a week without confronting the need for idea development. This is a widespread phenomenon, driven by strong, sometimes, global, market competition.

Innovation may also be demanded by other stakeholders in our work. A 2015 poll for Lithium Technologies showed that 65% of the US large-corporate executives report that consumers have higher expectations for them to innovate. Approximately 42% of respondents noted that consumers use social media to shame their company into doing what the consumer wants! 'The consumer is forever changed' asserts Rob Tarkoff, CEO and President.[7]

Also, the widespread and rapid proliferation of digital platforms has boosted change. Most organisations report that their digital initiatives are aimed at strengthening the existing business, rather than driving growth through new businesses. But don't doubt the short-term potential for digital becoming a source of value. In McKinsey's 2015 survey, their high-performing organisations are more than twice as likely to dedicate their best people and resources to their digital initiatives.[8]

And work problems seem to be growing in complexity. In their 2013 survey of 821 respondents across 14 countries, EY note that:

> Almost 9 out of 10 companies surveyed for this report agree that the problems confronting them are now so complex that teams are essential to provide effective solutions. To achieve superior performance, companies need to tap into the full range of skills and expertise at their disposal. More than 6 out of 10 respondents say that their companies' teams have become more diverse in the past three years and 55% say that their teams are more geographically distributed.[9]

One of the effects of this increased demand for ideas in organisations is that the search for ideas has broadened. Previously, innovation seemed to be the domain of people working in research, development, probably marketing and perhaps, sales. Now, ideas are needed from all the workforce, to develop new products and services, process efficiencies, start-up business models, new strategies and markets and more. This was foreseen:

> In the 21st-century world of electronically connected organizations, everyone will have a part to play as the creator and implementer of new

ideas. In this respect, older notions of the exceptional individual as a creative genius...will become obsolete.[10] (p. 55)

We're moving from creatively being a mysterious, even sacred, process, in the province of the few, to one which is becoming more widespread and more democratised.

As the conversational volume of organisational demand for innovation has increased, so is the demand from individuals. There is emerging a 'ground-up' drive from employees who want to learn the skills of idea development. This is disorganised and fragmented, and sometimes missed by their learning and development functions. But, what was a weak signal 10 years ago, is now growing more assuredly.

On a global professional services organisation learning programme that endured over 15 years, we ran client-skills training for young graduates. In 1:1 conversations, which typically roamed into considerations of skills, personal qualities, short and longer-term career considerations, these early-stage accountants, auditors, tax specialist and consultants increasingly enquired about opportunities for developing and applying their own creativity.

Often, their worry was that their role constrained their opportunities to demonstrate creativity. They were worried that their creative capability would shrink. Some wanted to live a more creative life. Some alluded to the routine and repetition in their role that denied them the opportunity to show imagination. Many wanted to do good work that developed the reputations of their clients and themselves. While a mix of motives was at play — personal and social — what was clear was that the demand for creativity was growing.

In a 2014 survey by Deloitte:

78 percent of Millennials were strongly influenced by how innovative a company was when deciding if they wanted to work there, but most say their current employer does not encourage them to think creatively.[11]

In his book *Working More Effectively with Millennials*, (people born after 1981), Karl Moore argues that, millennials have shifted strongly in their interests, away from a narrower pursuit of income, which he argues, characterised the 1980s and 1990s. Now they want to have more life balance, at work and home, and to contribute to something bigger than themselves. They want direction to aid their longer-term thinking and more purposeful work.[12]

They want their organisations to contribute to greater good. Specifically, they mention four global challenges: unemployment, resource scarcity, climate change/protecting the environment and income inequality. They also believe that business can, and should, aim to have positive impact in these areas. They see a role for business in creating new products and services to deliver benefits to broader society. In effect, they are challenging the limits of what their organisations are there to contribute.

One of the implications for large businesses is that millennials are loyal to purposeful work, but not to specific jobs in particular organisations. In one way, that's just as well, because there's another factor driving the demand for innovation skills.

Siu and Jaimovich released a paper in April 2015, describing how all employment gains in the US since 2001 have been in the area of non-routine work.[13] They categorised jobs as falling into one of four types. Routine roles are more 'rule-based' and divide into two types: routine manual (e.g. forklift operators, home appliance repairers), routine cognitive (e.g. book-keeping, bank tellers). Non-routine roles focus divide into non-routine manual, such as janitors and home health assistants, and non-routine cognitive, including programming and marketing. These contain fewer repetitive or rule-based activities, contain more variety within the role and require more flexibility (either cerebral or physical), and involve more human interaction, communication or decision-making discretion.

Their analysis shows that in economic recessions since 1990, routine roles have been falling in numbers, and not replaced with economic upturns. This trend accelerated after 2000. The authors conclude that this is partly because of outsourcing but mainly because these more routine roles are prime candidates to be replaced by new technologies such as robots and broad computing technology.

In the future, which jobs are more likely to need people? Martin Ford, futurist and author of *Rise of the Robots: Technology and the Threat of a Jobless Future*, argues that humans will be needed in the following three areas:

First, where human creativity is needed, such as in artistic and scientific work, and in developing new businesses strategies (although Ford cautions that none of us know how creative computers may become). Second, in roles where complex relationships are needed between people, and which require trust building. Examples include nursing, teaching, leading others and building client relationships. Third, Ford also includes work that is more unpredictable, such as a plumber who may receive calls to irregular locations at unpredictable times.[14]

The Wall Street Journal agrees with this broad argument:

> Even as robots become more skilled at more complex tasks, for decades to come it will be the province of humans to program and manage these machines. Many more jobs have critical elements that are creative, interpersonal, social and persuasive.[15]

No-one knows for sure how many and which jobs will be around in 2030. Most agree that the ones remaining will deliver value through creative and critical thinking, leadership, and the quality of human interaction.

My view is that part of the increased demand for broad innovation skills comes from people who foresee that these skills can, to some extent, safeguard their future. Add to this a desire for self-actualisation — creativity applied feels good! Plus, a growing wish to develop innovative approaches to benefit broader society. This is a considerable, collective, if fragmented, bottom-up force demanding that organisations develop their learning offerings around creativity, innovation and enterprise.

And where demand grows, supply is usually alongside. The number of courses offering learning in creativity, innovation and enterprise has rocketed in the last 10 years. A search on https://www.coursera.org/, a popular supplier of online courses, shows 200 offerings for the search term 'creativity', 261 for 'innovation' and 289 for 'enterprise'. These terms are well represented in a list of Coursera's 50 most popular courses in 2016.[16]

The need for innovation is also being driven at a more macro level. Meg Whitman, former CEO at HP Enterprise, wrote:

> We're now living in an Idea Economy where success is defined by the ability to turn ideas into value faster than your competition.[17]

Whitman's prescription can be scaled from team to country, especially when we start to note the prevalence of an increasingly educated workforce. In the USA, the percentage of the over-25 population with 4-year bachelor's degree, or higher, rose from 28% in 2007 to 33.4% in 2017. In the census bureau survey of 1940, just 4.6% said they had a 4-year degree.[18] In 2013, the proportion of working-age adults in the UK with a degree had more than doubled in two decades — rising to 38%. The same source claims that around 60% of the inner-London working population have a degree.[19]

We are developing better educated, idea-literate people, who care about the places where they live, and beyond, and want to make things better. And, while many pilot programmes are *ad hoc* and piecemeal, the broad move is towards greater involvement of more people in decision-making. For example, the Decide Madrid scheme was launched in 2015, aiming to give voters greater voice in local law and policy development.[20]

At national levels, for advanced Western societies, one of the challenges is how to deliver economic value without resorting to becoming countries of lowest-cost labour, and easily-substitutable production processes, whether of manufacturing or knowledge creation. In my view, countries will rely increasingly on the imagination and scalability of wealth-creating ideas. The working population's capacity to develop smart ideas, from initial insight to tested proposition, will become an increasingly-utilised item of social capital.

Delivering Innovation is Proving to be Difficult

While few contest that the need for innovation is growing, the quality of delivery seems to be lagging. Accenture's 2015 survey[21] of USA executives highlights that innovation performance does not match the rhetoric:

- Around 82% of respondents equate incremental performance improvement with more radical gains. While executives are stating a need for more radical change, the great majority of changes improve what is already there.
- Furthermore, and worryingly, 60% admit their companies do not learn from past mistakes (compared to 36% in 2012).
- About 67% believe their organisations are more risk averse (versus 46% in 2012).

The report argues that the discipline of innovation is in a state of rapid development. They note the increasing number of chief innovation officers (up to 63%, from 54% in 2009); of formal processes for idea development (74%, compared to 62% in 2012); 86% use ideation platforms to support collaboration with internal and external stakeholders, with 91% noting that customers are a valuable source of new ideas. Clearly, USA organisations are experimenting with formalising support structures for innovation. Part of the challenge may be in developing an integrated approach. The same report concludes that:

> ...these enabling technologies can do little on their own. They need to be part of a clear innovation strategy and support well defined innovation processes to be most effective.

The link to strategy is important. Wazoku is a growing, UK-based open innovation business. Their 2015 survey, invited views from executives through to frontline UK workers. Its results are arresting:

> Over 90% of those we spoke to said improving customer experience and making cost savings were two of the most important strategic objectives for their employees. 85% agreed these areas could be improved through more innovative ideas and approaches, but almost the same amount stated innovation ambiguity and barriers meant this benefit is unlikely to ever be realized (80%).[22]

While organisations are experimenting, and rapidly, with new approaches to innovation, an interesting *Forbes* article gives an insight as to the possible effect on employees. The article discusses a survey from MindMatters and shares that:

> Only 5% of respondents report that workers in innovation programs feel highly motivated to innovate. More than three of four say their new ideas are poorly reviewed and analysed... The lack of recognition for contributions to innovation is also striking: almost half (49%) believe they won't receive any benefit or recognition for developing successful ideas.[23]

All of this points to an innovation truism: it is easier to state the need for innovation than deliver it. Indeed, our understanding of how ideas actually develop in real time, with real people on real work, is decidedly patchy:

> There are remarkably few studies of change that actually allow the change process to reveal itself in any kind of substantially temporal or contextual manner…episodic views of change not only treat innovations as if they had a clear beginning and a clear end but also, where they limit themselves to snapshot time-series data, fail to provide data on the mechanisms and processes through which change are created.[24] (pp. 93–94).

Innovation and Reification

It is clear that the need for innovation has been growing, while the process of delivering it is fragmented, experimental and poorly understood. What's more, we humans have a tendency to use concepts that are simultaneously convenient and distancing. Reification is one process by which we achieve this. It refers to our tendency to make something 'real' — to objectify and make phenomena into a thing. For example, we may conceive ideas as moving upstream through various stages of the innovation process — from someone's initial insight about a market need, to the acceptance of a genuine problem, to the building of solutions that might solve the problem, and so on. The imagery, like fish moving upstream, is captivating.

We talk as if ideas were real, tangible entities. If we're fortunate, the products and services they eventually yield might be. But ideas are convenient concepts around which we may find common agreement, to aid discussion. They act as psychological 'holding mechanisms', to frame our attention.

The downside of our tendency to reify phenomena is that we lose an understanding of how innovation actually happens in organisations. Birdi *et al.*, note this lack of understanding of how ideas are actually developed within organisations. They make the powerful point that it is not economies or sectors that innovate but individual firms within them. They go on to state that 'opening the black box' of the firm and understanding how innovation really works can help countries as a whole, through enhancing positive trends and reversing negative ones.[25]

I'd extend their point further to state that it is some people within organisations that innovate. Most people's everyday experience of life in organisations relates to being part of conversations. Some of these are repetitive, stale and risk averse. Others revolve around possibilities for doing something new. Many conversations combine patterns of repetition with glimpses of the new. If we can become more attuned to how conversations develop between people, then we're getting nearer to sensing how innovation succeeds.

Our tendency to reification can blind us to the everyday realities faced by people trying to innovate in their work. What we gain in linguistic convenience, we lose in empathy with innovators.

The Innovation Bind

A corollary of working on complex challenges that require creative solutions, developed through imagination, is that no-one knows these solutions in advance! Assuming that a group has agreed the problem, the process can be thought of this way.[26]

We might think: 'If we're doing something *new* to our context, there are no obvious "right" answers and we have to accept uncertainty, ambiguity and surprises along the way. This is exciting and liberating…how can we possibly go wrong? There is no "wrong" — only possibilities…'

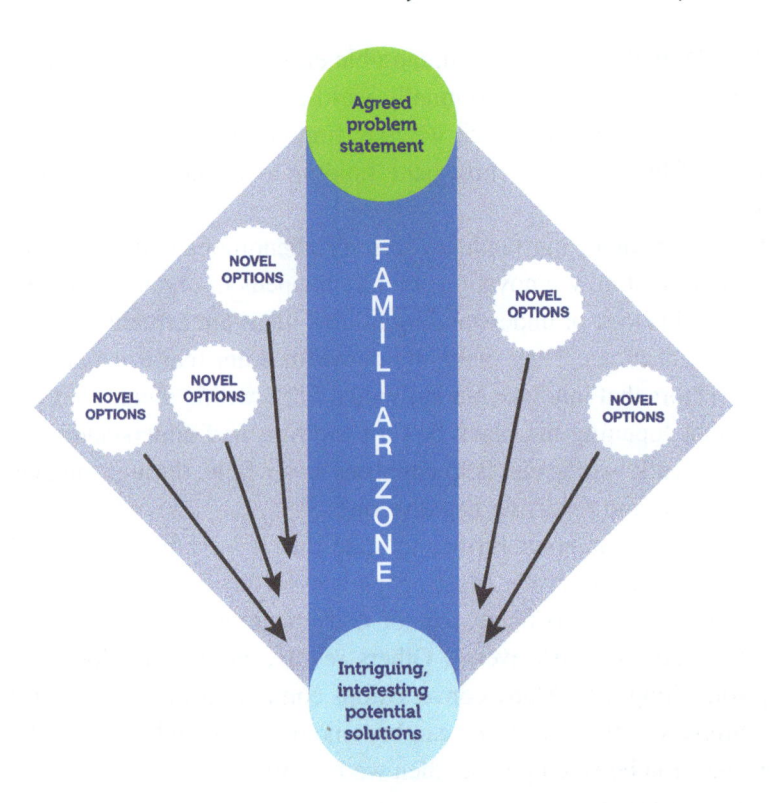

Figure 1.1: Incorporating novelty (Adapted from Ref. [26])

But this not knowing can also bring anxiety, which, can be a strong force for closing down our perception, feeling and thinking. Through experiencing processes of research and consulting with groups, there seem to be work environment factors which are experienced by people, in ways that lead us back to the road of the more familiar, and away from the novelty that is needed (see Figure 1.1).

> There is a wealth of evidence to confirm the common impression that when people feel threatened, pressurised, judged or stressed, they tend to revert to ways of thinking that are more clear-cut, more tried and tested, and more conventional: in a word, less creative.[27] (p. 76)

This was supported by Goleman and Boyatzis[28] who describe how chronic stress increases cortisol and adrenaline levels affect memory, planning and creativity. In short, these thinking processes narrow down, reducing our quality of exploration and returning people to habitual thinking.

Broadly, there seem to be a series of factors that are unhelpful for creativity:

- High uncertainty about desired outcomes and/or working process. Too much uncertainty of information and ambiguity about the meaning of messages.
- Too high a workload, and too little resource, can lead to the feeling of being on the proverbial treadmill, rushing from one deadline to another. In the UK, at least, the perception is that we are also working longer hours. And more of us believe our productivity has reduced rather than increased.[29]
- The perceived threat of evaluation and potential exposure if the work is perceived to 'fail'. This is closely linked with a perceived lack of support from more senior leadership.
- Poor work relationships across the work units concerned, reducing trust and perceived psychological safety.

Any of these factors can generate an anxiety that limits exploration and imagination. In combination, they are exponentially more likely to lead people to withdraw their energies and avoid any risk taking. When people feel like this, teams weed out novel ideas, leaving the safer ones that are likely to be palatable to powerful, more senior people.

What is striking is that several of these factors seem to be on the increase: the demand for innovation, in sectors with increased regulation, and increased involvement from stakeholders like consumers, clients, parents, carers, families, etc., add to this the existence of social media and the potential for widespread public criticism is increased. It can build a negative anticipation that leads people to retreat and seek safety.

This is the bind: the very factors contributing to the need for innovation may provide the uncertainties and pressures that can make this thinking difficult. They are examples of the confluence of emergent, complex trends in society, planned by no one, but powerful all the same.

But innovation outcomes are not inevitable. What helps groups continue to explore, and why, sometimes, does it all fall apart?

On the client-skills learning programme I mentioned earlier, our team was helping young graduates to learn about client-management skills. Typically, a programme would involve 18 participants over two days working in three groups of six people. Each group would work with a facilitator whose role was to help people learn aspects of client management, and, aim to raise their awareness of, and maximise, their personal strengths. A feature of the 2-day programme was that we worked with UK charities who would provide real work challenges for our participants. Examples included:

- 'We have a publicity event in 6 months, and are including auction lots — please find us two auction lots that people couldn't find elsewhere'.
- 'Help us refine our marketing and promotions strategy'.
- 'Help us raise new sources of funds because our previous ones are "drying up"'.

Quite often, the challenges were open ended and charity clients encouraged the course participants to generate as many unusual ideas as possible, and sometimes, highly original ones. In working with the group of six over two days, I observed how they worked together. There were two aspects to their work: one was the charity task itself — providing some value to the client; the other was the more nebulous work concerned with participants learning something about the skills of client management which may build transferable skills for their ongoing practice.

As facilitator, my role was to stop the group working solely on the task and help them reflect both on their current task and their personal learning. With one team, I noted that:

There was a limited diversity in this team, as judged by a measure of interpersonal preference style. There was some discussion of 'what we are expected to do here', but this was not sustained. The groups stuck with what the client has asked for — not clarifying or challenging it. Anxiety levels are high throughout much of day 2. The more the course progressed, the higher the anxiety levels and the less prepared was the group to stop and reflect on its way of working. There was little psychological safety in the room. I felt a palpable sense of the group wishing to be left to 'get on with it'. As a facilitator, my presence was unwelcome, because, I think, I brought an uncomfortable reminder of the other things the group should be considering. Even though the group may have believed its output was mediocre — as the client later remarked — they also perceived it was too late to start again. The more anxiety rose, the lower became psychological safety, reflexivity and group efficacy, and the stronger became the cornered fixation on task: 'rabbits in the deadline headlights'.[30]

But it wasn't always this way. Innovation was sometimes experienced as exciting, challenging, ripe for exploration, with the opportunity to learn new approaches. When there was trust and a sense of psychological safety between group members, then there tended to be more open sharing of ideas, and joint development of ideas, and better use of differences within groups. And, if the group is supported in its innovative work by more senior people, this gives a 'safety net', knowing they can't go far wrong. On this programme, I tried to do this, as the facilitator, and I encouraged the charity clients to do the same. With another group, the story was different:

> ...the quality of direct, frank communication was remarkable. One member of this group — L — was sincere in asking for honest feedback from others in the team. His directness was shown in both asking for feedback on his performance, and giving others feedback on their own. The effect in the group was to 'up' the challenge for all of us. Others rose to this challenge, and the quality of their communication and feedback increased to rare levels. The mood in the group changed for the better, as people realised that something unusual was happening. The quality of discussion rose sharply. Once achieved, people wanted more of this. What was happening, as far as I was concerned, was that a sense of excitement filled the room. People knew that the others were taking time and effort to help them with their learning goals, and trust in the group was high. There was little of the hedging, generalising and being careful that often reflects the climate of a group where trust is lower. The effect was to 'buck-up'

everyone, as people felt a mutual obligation to 'go out on a limb' and tell others what they'd done well and could have done better.[31]

This group were prepared to take remarkable risks with their learning. In a short time, they achieved a rare level of mutual support and openness. They learnt new and significant things about themselves, and they'd done this in rapid time.

A *Cri de Coeur* for the Age of Creativity

The opportunity is that this could be a golden age for creativity, with leaders acting as catalysts, accelerating group processes. But, evidently, times are challenging. There are four governing issues here:

First, while technology reshapes our world of work, so the demand for, and supply of, creativity capabilities is growing. These different trends, for efficiency and creativity, provide a present-day tension felt across many societies. Two men, born within two years of each other in the 1850s, would have recognised the pattern. Frederick Taylor, the founder of so-called Scientific Management, was born in Germantown, Philadelphia on 20 March 1856. One of the principles of Scientific Management was to increase the efficiencies of work methods, by studying and training workers in the 'one best way' to do the job. Typically, this led to a specialised division of labour, such that unskilled workers could learn their part of the workflow well enough for overall productivity to soar. Scientific Management was largely a convergent process: identify the best approach; organise and equip workers to be able to carry this out in the most efficient way; and monitor for adherence.

Once the variability of the human factor is lowered, Taylor's approach gives the promise of more predictable work methods. (Indeed, he seems to have had an abiding concern around control and predictability. At the age of 12, and suffering from nightmares, he invented a harness to prevent himself from sleeping on his back.)[31] His work has been widely applied and hugely influential, but what Taylor did not foresee was that the practice of deskilling work would lead to increasingly easy substitution of workers. Once work was deskilled and broken down into simple components, it might be carried out by anyone, rather than an originally skilled craftworker; then by offshoring, as globalisation allowed for work to carried out on other continents; and finally, by automation, as routine tasks might be performed by non-humans.

Graham Wallas was born two years later, in Monkwearmouth, near Sunderland, UK on 31 May 1858. He was a social psychologist, educationalist and a co-founder of the London School of Economics and Political Science. He also produced an early and influential articulation of the stages of the creative process in his 1926 book, *The Art of Thought*.[32]

Wallas outlined four stages of the creative process — preparation, incubation, illumination and verification — and we'll look at these more in Chapter 4. One of the interesting aspects of his work was his insight that creativity cannot be rushed, and that we weave an elegant path, through the interplay of conscious and unconscious thoughts. As an educator, he was also stating that these steps can be learnt. Wallas would be excited by the current increase in demand for creativity skills. He would also sense the opportunities for a more systematic approach to learning these skills.

Second, there is a hype phenomenon. Innovation, of course, is not a new concept. What is new is the breadth and depth of expectation. It seems as if innovation has become the prescription for most of our organisational and societal ills. The word is applied freely to the need for new products, services, processes, business models, strategies, markets, cost-efficiencies; in degrees from incremental to radical, disruptive and breakthrough. It sounds like a secular promise that can deliver us from the perils of stagnation and declining living standards.

However, right now, the need for innovation is most certainly not ingrained into employees' everyday work. The innovation volume is turned high, but there is a gulf between the shouting and most people's everyday, lived experience. The overworked in our societies may experience this growing demand as yet another pressure on their already-overloaded selves. Cynicism and suspicion are relatively easy states to activate. It would be easy to dismiss innovation as another over-hyped, groundless concept. Those of us involved in innovation education need faith and resilience.

Third, there are grounds for optimism. For example, we already know a lot about learning the skills of creativity. Research and teaching have been carried out fairly systematically since the late 1960s, and we look at this through Chapters 3–6. Focusing on these metacapabilities makes educational sense:

> Lifelong learning starts at school. As a rule, education should not be narrowly vocational. The curriculum needs to teach children how to study and think. A focus on "metacognition" will make them better at picking up skills later in life.[33]

Creative thinking is one such metacognition — a skill in thinking about how to think. I explain in Chapter 4 how creativity skills include the capacity for both divergent and convergent thinking. Traditional school and workplace education tends to focus more on the latter. Both are learnable. And creative thinking is not setting specific. It has the potential for being applied across occupations, meaning that it can be an aid for multi-disciplinary working and collaboration within and across organisations.

Another source for optimism is that organisations can be pioneers of learning which shape international conversations. More so than most governments, universities, and public bodies, our small, medium and large organisations are developing new ways of delivering value.

And there is potential for a 'spread' factor, led from the ground up. With increasingly educated populations, people are transferring their learning from work to other domains of their lives, such as their communities and cities. Work learning can have a multiplier effect, as it ripples into other areas of our lives.

Finally, as I aim to show through the examples in this book, good learning is already happening. Leaders are acting as innovation catalysts by thinking carefully about the power they have, and acting in mature ways to engage and involve others around a purposeful change. As we'll see in the next chapter, doing so requires the leader to work with the team, not above them.

References

1. Edelman, R. (2017). Edelman Trust Barometer. Available at: https://www.edelman.com/p/6-a-m/an-implosion-of-trust/ (Accessed: 23/12/2017).
2. Schumpeter, J. A. (2011). *The Economist*. Available at: https://www.economist.com/node/21525350 (Accessed 23/10/2011).
3. Gryskiewicz, S. (1987). Predictable Creativity. In: *Frontiers of Creativity Research: Beyond the Basics* by S. G. Isaksen, (Ed.), pp. 305–313. Buffalo, NY: Bearly.
4. West, M. A. and Anderson, N. R. (1996). "Innovation in Top Management Teams." *Journal of Applied Psychology* 81(6): 680–693.
5. Isaksen, S. G., Dorval, B. D., and Treffinger, D. J. (2011). *Creative Approaches to Problem Solving: A Framework for Innovation and Change*. 3rd edition. Thousand Oaks, CA: Sage.
6. Rhodes, M. (1961). "An Analysis of Creativity." *Phi, Delta, Kappan* 42: 305–310.
7. Press department (2015). Lithium. Available at: http://www.lithium.com/company/news-room/press-releases/2015/corporate-america-under-pressure-from-consumers-rising-expectations) (Accessed: 10/10/2016).
8. Bughin, J. *et al.* (2015). McKinsey. Available at: https://www.mckinsey.com/business-functions/digital-mckinsey/our-insights/cracking-the-digital-code (Accessed on 20/09/2016).
9. EY (2013). Available at: http://www.ey.com/gl/en/issues/talent-management/how-companies-use-teams-to-drive-performance (Accessed on 21/09/2016).
10. West, M. and Rickards, T. (1999). Innovation. Vol. 2. In: *Encyclopedia of Creativity* by Pritzker, S. and Runco, M. (Eds.), pp. 45–55. San Diego: Academic Press.
11. Deloitte (2014). Available at: https://www2.deloitte.com/content/dam/Deloitte/ru/Documents/Corporate_responsibility/ru_2014_MillennialSurvey_ExecutiveSummary.pdf (Accessed on 28/10/2016).
12. Moore, K. (2014). *Forbes*. Available at: http://www.forbes.com/sites/karlmoore/2014/10/02/millennials-work-for-purpose-not-paycheck/ (Accessed on: 01/10/2016).
13. Siu, H. and Jaimovich, N. (2015). Third Way. Available at: http://www.thirdway.org/report/jobless-recoveries (Accessed on 08/01/2017).
14. Davies, D. (2015). NPR. Available at: https://www.npr.org/sections/alltechconsidered/2015/05/18/407648886/attention-white-collar-workers-the-robots-are-coming-for-your-jobs (Accessed on 09/01/2017).

15. Zumbrun, J. (2015). *Wall Street Journal*. Available at: https://blogs.wsj.com/economics/2015/04/08/is-your-job-routine-if-so-its-probably-disappearing/ (Accessed on 09/02/2017).
16. Pearce, K. (2016). DIY Genius. Available at: https://www.diygenius.com/the-50-most-popular-courses-on-coursera/ (Accessed on 13/03/2017).
17. Whitman, M. (2015). Linkedin. Available at: https://www.linkedin.com/pulse/state-technology-welcome-idea-economy-meg-whitman/ (Accessed on 11/11/2016).
18. Wilson, R. (2017). The Hill. Available at: http://thehill.com/homenews/state-watch/326995-census-more-americans-have-college-degrees-than-ever-before (Accessed on 03/04/2017).
19. Coughlan, S. (2013). BBC. Available at: www.bbc.co.uk/news/education-25002401 (Accessed on 13/14/2017).
20. Simon, J. *et al.* (2017). NESTA. Available at: https://www.nesta.org.uk/publications/digital-democracy-tools-transforming-political-engagement (Accessed on 11/11/2017).
21. Alon, A. and Elron, D. (2015). Accenture. Available at: https://www.accenture.com/us-en/insight-innovation-survey-clear-vision-cloudy-execution (Accessed on 03/08/2017).
22. Hill, S. and Beswick, C. (2016). Wazoku. Available at: https://www.wazoku.com/resource/everyday-innovation-report/ (Accessed on 11/11/2017).
23. Denning, S. (2015). *Forbes*. Available at: https://www.forbes.com/sites/stevedenning/2015/02/27/is-there-an-innovation-crisis-at-us-firms/#148092b564cb (Accessed on 09/09/2017).
24. Pettigrew, A. M. (1995). Longitudinal Field Research on Change. Vol. 1. In: *Longitudinal Field Research Methods: Studying Processes of Organizational Change* by Van de Ven, A. H. and Huber, G. P. (Eds.), pp. 91–125. Thousand Oaks, CA: Sage.
25. Birdi, K. S., Denyer, D., Munir, K., Pradhu, J. and Neely, A. (2003). "Post Porter: Where does the UK Go From Here?" *Aim Management Research Forum*.
26. Puccio, G. J., Murdock, M. C. and Mance, M. (2007). *Creative Leadership: Skills that Drive Change*. Thousand Oaks, CA: Sage.
27. Claxton, G. (1998). *Hare Brain, Tortoise Mind: Why Intelligence Increases When You Think Less*. London: Fourth Estate.
28. Goleman, D. and Boyatzis, R. (2008). "Social Intelligence and the Biology of Leadership." *Harvard Business Review*, September: 74–81.
29. Inman, P. (2016). *The Guardian*. Available at: https://www.theguardian.com/business/2016/mar/27/britons-working-longer-hours-with-no-gain-in-

productivity-study-finds?_ga=2.16443891.454952020.1506367755-1374511110.1506367755 (Accessed on 10/11/2017).
30. Sheffield, R. (2012). Understanding the complex organizational processes that help and hinder creativity and innovation. Unpublished PHd thesis.
31. Copley, F. (1923). *Frederick W. Taylor, Father of Scientific Management*, Vol. 2. Manhattan: Harper and Brothers.
32. Wallas, G. (1926). *The Art of Thought*. New York: Harcourt, Brace and Company.
33. *The Economist* (2017). Available at: https://www.economist.com/news/leaders/21714341-it-easy-say-people-need-keep-learning-throughout-their-careers-practicalities (Accessed on 19/09/2017).

Chapter 2

Rethinking Power and Leadership

> Nearly all men can stand adversity, but if you want to test a man's character, give him power.
>
> **Abraham Lincoln**

My first job was in the British Coal Industry, in 1987. My immediate manager, John, was very competent, utterly focused and shouted quite a lot. I'm sure he had high blood pressure. In the late 1980s and early 1990s, the publishing industry was different, with more female senior leaders. But the same taken-for-granted expectations existed: leaders wanted their orders to be carried out, and their authority was largely unquestioned. Broadly, the operating assumption was that good leaders knew what to do, and they'd focus their teams as needed. Work itself was fairly routine and predictable, and power was invested in individual leaders.

It has been a different story since then. People in leadership roles were embedded in their wider societies. As the world was changing, so were our conceptions of leaders' roles and our expectations of our interactions with them. Culturally, the norms have changed. We are less accepting of the authority of leaders, whether in the business or governmental realms. It has been an age of gradually advancing openness and inclusivity in many societies.

The role of coaching has expanded around the globe. Coaching is, essentially, an inclusive leadership style aimed at accelerating the development of others. And many people want their leader to help them with their job and career development. For many leaders, these cultural changes have had the effect of changing their conception of their roles.

For many, the nature of work itself seems to have changed. As Chapter 1 shows, work has become more complex, requiring diverse teams to come together to solve more complex problems. More stakeholders want a say in what constitutes 'success'. Most markets are more turbulent and competitive, and product and service cycle times have shortened in many sectors.

Technologically, we created the digital world of emails, Internet and social media platforms. (To remember a time before emails seems unutterably quaint. For me, it was sometime around 1995.) In short time, we have become a content-producing society, able to connect billions of people on the planet, and reduce the time gap from thought to sharing. Increased access to, and transparency of, information has meant that more of us have come to expect a 'voice' in our work. The leader can't control access to information, and is unlikely to be the first to hear significant market, customer or organisational information.

Individual leaders certainly don't have all the answers to these complex challenges of work. Broadly, the shift of focus has been away from the individual leader, and to one who understands that their role has become one of connecting their people to each other, information and to important agendas in organisations.

The above shift could be interpreted as a decline in the importance of leadership. If anything, the opposite is true. Year after year, the challenge of developing effective leaders is a top corporate, strategic challenge. Leadership development is a $130 billion global market.[1]

Research Overview: Power and Leadership

While the development of creative ideas might be carried out by individuals, or groups from within or beyond the organisation, innovation is usually a more political and social process. Since innovation will involve the implementation of something novel, in order to bring benefits, there is an inherent degree of unpredictability. For unpredictability, read 'risk' as those with power might have to accept a loss of control over processes and outcomes. Idea implementation typically needs the support of powerful people, which can manifest as the more explicit forms of formal allocation of time, people and financial resources, as well as the 'softer' sorts of leaders' attention, encouragement, sponsorship and coaching.

Organisational changes affect people's work relationships and networks, status and rewards packages. No wonder change arouses a mix of emotions. Yet, power and politics have been largely marginalised in creativity and innovation research.[2] This is partly because very little research in this area has been conducted with real teams, in real time, as they develop ideas from initial insights to implementation testing. Such empirical research is time consuming, can be difficult to access, and with research conditions hard to control. It's much easier to set up short experiments with a group of students.

But difficulty is not the only reason. In his trilogy on Cicero, the Roman lawyer, Robert Harris says that Cicero never talked about power, despite the novels focusing imaginatively on the intimate social processes by which Cicero gained, maintained and, eventually, lost power and influence in the governing of Rome.

The same can be said of contemporary discussions of power in leadership. Leaders very rarely talk explicitly about the power they have. How power is acquired, maintained and lost is sometimes the proverbial elephant in the room. And it is inherent to the innovation process.

In Chapter 1, I described briefly the crisis of trust in leadership reported through the annual Edelman survey. Over the time of writing this book, society has witnessed various high-profile abuses of power that have further diminished the reputation of leaders as individuals, and leadership as a calling.

The German car company, VW, admitted to cheating diesel emissions tests in the US, through installing software that deliberately changed performance results. The repercussions of the reported BBC gender pay differences are still unravelling. Victims reported long-term sexual abuse and harassment by men, of women, in the entertainment and political spheres, leading to the #timesup and #metoo campaigns. While these examples are different in many ways, they are also perceived to have a common aspect: that of the preservation, and misuse, of power, by those with power. And while people may forget details of specific cases, what lingers is the abiding impression of power misuse.

Dr. Karen Blakeley is the Head of the Centre for Responsible Management at Winchester University. She advocates that leaders, and potential leaders, consider embracing power in the service of a higher purpose, extending beyond our personal interests. She reminds us that:

> At the core of responsible leadership lies purpose — what are we exercising leadership for? Somehow our business leaders seem to have got their priorities skewed. The WWF Living Planet Report of 2015 reminds us: 'Ecosystems sustain societies that create economies. It does not work any other way round'.[3] (p. 146)

In conversation for this book, we discussed the topic of power and how leaders think about, talk about and use power:

> …According to my experience, I don't think leaders understand enough about the different kinds of power, and the different conceptualisations of power. I don't think it's talked about enough actually…I think it's probably the most important thing that executives need to think about… They have power, like it or not; they don't understand the extent of the power they have, how they're using it, the impact of it, and how to maximize it for good aims.

Dr. Blakeley goes on to argue that leadership and power are inextricable, can be compatible, and require more public discussion:

> The embracing of power as responsible leaders in the context of conscience, good purpose, love, awareness and service is one of the most important ways we can address the crisis of leadership in our own time. How we embrace power is a challenging question. For those to whom power feels natural and attractive, this practice may be about developing greater humility and seeking honest feedback from others. For those who baulk at taking power, the practice may involve learning to recognise and utilise power for a higher purpose.[3] (p. 147)

What Dr. Blakeley is referring to is highly topical but is not new. When the Harvard psychologist David McClelland wrote *Power, the Inner*

Experience in 1975, he reflected on why young Americans (men — it was 1975) are not attracted to powerful roles in society:

> My own view is that young people avoid socio-political leadership roles...because in our society in our time, and perhaps in all societies at all times, the exercise of power is viewed negatively. People are suspicious of a man who wants power, even if he does so for sincere and altruistic reasons. He is often socially conditioned to be suspicious of himself. Since he does not want to be in a position where he might be thought to be seeking power in order to exploit others, he shuns public responsibility.[4] (p. 256)

From reimagining Cicero to current times, power remains an evasive concept. But it is also a core aspect of leadership, and an essential aspect of innovation. And McClelland was part of a groundbreaking research movement that helped us understand power in much more depth. The research has implications for leadership in the innovation context. And McClelland's work also has the potential to help us reimagine the power in ways more palatable to our times.

Before understanding the implications for leadership, some background on the research itself is necessary. In the late 1940s, McClelland worked with graduate student, John Atkinson, to research psychological motives. McClelland was particularly interested in how our unconscious thoughts affected our behaviours, and our lack of awareness of the strength of these unconscious thoughts. He later attributed the source of his interest in the unconscious to his childhood experiences of the lack of consistency between the values people avowed in Sunday church and their actual behaviours through the rest of the week.[5]

There are methodological challenges in understanding what people are thinking about in a given situation, when those people themselves are unaware! What the researchers found was that the best way to do this was by asking people to write brief, imaginative stories of pictures they'd been given by the researchers. This was called the thematic apperception test (later renamed the Picture Stories Exercise), and developed by Morgan and Murray in 1935. While writing these fantasy stories the person does not know what is being measured, and simply writes in response to the picture stimuli. The thought content reflects what is on the mind at the moment, and recurring themes of thoughts were called 'motives'. McClelland argued that this method is highly sensitive to revealing changes in our motives.

Through the late 1940s and into the 1950s, researchers found there to be hundreds of different motives in existence in humans. Work studies tended to focus more on achievement, affiliation and power, because of the relevance of these to personal, organisational and societal advancement. As research developed between the 1950s and 1970s, scoring systems for all three motives were devised so that people's motive levels could be measured with confidence. Many studies later, these three motive systems are still relevant concepts for academics and practitioners.

In essence, the achievement motive is concerned with standards and improvement. The person high in this will think, fantasise, talk, write about and act on situations in which s/he does things better. Gratification comes from the feeling of reward from channelling one's energy in a context where results show that improvement is down to personal effort. Studies have shown that this motive is important for economic development in countries. For example, successful start-ups often need a high degree of this thought — it drives behaviours that result in measurable improvement. Entrepreneurs strong in this can be good at judging the risk of task accomplishment. As companies grow, these same people can struggle to shift their role from a task manager to a people manager. For them, the temptation is to do the work themselves. Influencing others is a different, and often difficult, matter.

The affiliation motive is different and revolves around the formation, maintenance and repair of social relationships. People who are strong in this motive will, consciously and unconsciously, think about their relationships. And, as with the other motives, their thoughts will drive their actions. Litwin and Siebrecht found that in so-called integrative, managerial roles, better performance was associated with higher affiliation.[6] The employee relations manager's role revolved around enabling management and unions to talk to each other productively. Since people high in affiliation think about repairing and maintaining relationships, the demands of the role seem to fit their already-prevailing thought patterns.

But too high an affiliation need can be a hindrance in most leadership roles, where the emphasis is on performance improvement. With affiliation goes the preference to avoid conflict, and the leader high in affiliation may well make exceptions for individual circumstances. Others in the group are likely to perceive these exceptions as being unfair, which leads to a poor morale. Hence, the leader's wish to keep the 'peace' leads directly to the opposite.

The power motive is most relevant for this book. As research deepened in this concept, through the 1950s into the 1970s, and the motive system itself became clearer, so the power motive became understood as a cluster of thoughts, all directed around feeling strong and powerful. People strong in the power motive, tend to think, consciously and unconsciously, and more so than others, about ways of interacting with their social environment with the outcome being that they feel strong and powerful. They think about having impact either on themselves or on others.

The research concept itself has been very resilient and its myriad manifestations have been studied in contexts of risk taking, alcohol consumption, war, physiological functioning, health and leadership.[7]

Before we look at the link between the power motive and leadership, the researchers also discovered something very important: the same level of power motive across different people might be expressed through very different behaviours. For some it may involve directly influencing others, through powerful actions, such as persuading or helping; for another person it might involve having a drink; for another it entails dieting or exercise; or for another, the feeling of strength comes from strong association with others. As McClelland put it: different actions, same effect: feeling of power.

In 1973, ground-breaking research from Abigail Stewart helped us understand more about the development of the power motive, and why it can be channelled in different ways for different people.[8] Hers is a model of social-emotional maturity, represented in Table 2.1, and elaborated upon in the McClelland's *Power: The Inner Experience*.

In stage 1, the person is the target of power, and the source is others. For example, a child needs food, drink and love from a carer in order to feel satisfied. This stage is called dependence because the source of power is external to the target of power. Praise from authority figures may provide us with a sense of feeling powerful, but so might drugs and alcohol. In a leadership context, people who have a strong component of stage 1

Table 2.1: Source and target of power

		Source of Power	
		Others	*Self*
Target of Power	*Self*	Stage 1: Dependence	Stage 2: Independence
	Others	Stage 4: Interdependent	Stage 3: Assertive A: Personal B: Institutional

power do not want leadership positions. Instead, they feel powerful through their association with powerful others. The label of dependent will be uncomfortable for people strong in this stage. They do not see themselves as being dependent. Instead, they see themselves as being strong through being near an external source of strength.

Stage 2 is labelled independence because the source and target of power are the same: the self. The child turns away their head from food when it is offered. The adult might gather prestige possessions such as credit cards, cars, smartphones, all of which can make the person feel stronger and more independent of adult control. Alternatively, the adult may become stronger through behaviours such as dieting and exercise that show self-management and willpower. In the leadership realm, individuals high in independence don't want to lead others and they don't want to be led.

Stage 3 is labelled assertive because the flow of power is from the individual out to others. The subject is the source, others are the target. As the child grows, he finds that an alternative way of feeling powerful is to influence, even control, others. In an organisational context, these expressions become modified to more subtle techniques such as negotiating, bargaining and controlling the behaviour of others in more palatable ways. The act of having impact on others makes the person feel strong and powerful. There are two sub-categories here, depending on the goal of the influence.

Stage 3A describes individuals who used power for their personal goals. They usually did not have the patience or discipline to build institutional influence. They may express their power in more impulsive ways, even aggressive. Their concern seems to be to win in competitive situations. Experience suggests that leaders strong in personal power tend to surround themselves with loyal followers, whom they then reward, in return for loyalty to the leader's agenda, rather than for loyalty to wider organisational aims. Work matters tend to become more political than performance oriented. When these leaders leave their roles, they often leave a trail of discord and a team in tatters.

Stage 3B describes institutional leaders. The research found that these leaders thought about, and used, power differently to those at the personal power stage. They were more inhibited about using power. Their thoughts expressed wishes to exercise power for the benefit of others, and an ambivalence in exercising their own strength, realising, for example, that every victory is someone else's loss. As we'll see below, leaders strong in this stage of the power motive often made good organisational leaders. They allied their thinking about influencing others with the discipline to do so in pursuit of organisational goals.

Stage 4 leadership is labelled interdependent. Again, the goal state for people who think a lot about power motivation is the same: to feel strong and powerful. However, the route to doing so, and the impact on others, is profoundly different. At this stage, people act as a conduit to helping others feel strong. They are open to being influenced by others and they influence others. They are generally less concerned with their own ego, and they often wish to serve a worthwhile cause. As with stage 3, they tend to accept leadership positions and the power that goes with this. They are aware of the importance of engaging their team fully, and that they, as leader, certainly don't have all the answers. The leader strong in this stage of power is with their team, rather than above them.

The model developed by McClelland, Stewart and others was a more thorough elaboration of power. McClelland's strong point was that academics and potential leaders had conflated power with stage 3A, personal power, as described above. But, as he describes, there are more socialised ways of channelling the power motive, so that leaders and followers can feel inspired to pursue goals for the good of society. And this type of 'power' rarely gets discussed:

> One leads people by helping them set their goals, by communicating widely through the group, and by taking the initiative in formulating means of achieving the goals, and finally, by inspiring members of the

group to work hard for those goals. Such an image of the exercise of power and influence in a leadership role should not frighten anyone, and should convince people that power exercised in this way is not only not dangerous but of the greatest possible use to society.[4] (p. 268)

The rehabilitation of power was one of McClelland's goals. Another was to apply psychological learning to help leaders become more effective. The following section shows how there has been a shift in what constitutes effective leadership over a generation, with the power motive at the heart of the debate.

Training in the Power Motive

In 1976, David McClelland and David Burnham looked at the performance results of a range of more than 500 leaders from 25 US corporations.[9] They defined performance in this context as a combination of team climate, as measured by team members and sales performance data.

McClelland and Burnham found that people strong in the power motive tend to be attracted to positions of power. But the power motive, by itself, wasn't enough to predict superior performance in the role. They found that more successful leaders shared a motive pattern

- as well as being strong in the power motive — wishing to influence and have impact on others — the successful leaders also shared a strong sense of inhibition. They channelled their power into socialised goals, for the good of the organisation, rather than personal goals for themselves. From our previous stage model, they were expressing 3B: institutional power;
- their affiliation motive was lower than their power motive. In other words, their need to have impact was greater than their need to be liked.

McClelland and Burnham labelled these institutional leaders because they aimed to build and serve the institutions to which they belonged. These leaders were certainly interested in influence, but not in manipulating their team members for their own ends. Quite the contrary. The 3B institutional leaders made their team members feel strong. Whereas the 3A personal power leaders lacked the discipline to build sustainable institutions. When they left, the people left behind did not know what to do.

And the results of the institutional leaders were impressive. They built healthier working climates, as measured by their own team members. And team climate was shown to be a 'lead' indicator of sales results. The higher the team climate earlier in the year, the higher were sales at the end of the year.

McClelland believed that motives were able to change quite readily. He'd already successfully trained Indian entrepreneurs to develop their achievement motive.[10] For the power motive, he and his researchers developed the social technology of power motive training to help people understand how the power motive affected thought, action and outcomes in their role. They trained 194 community action agency officers — people with local community influencing roles. These people learnt the 3B institutional socialised mode of power, as it seemed most relevant to their work — in developing their levels of influence to help poor, local people in their communities. Interview evaluations showed that 60% of the trainees had improved their performance some months after training, becoming better organisers and influencers in their communities.[7]

In the same sales leadership study described above, McClelland and Burnham trained sales leaders from 16 districts across the USA to strengthen their socialised power motive. The first evaluation gathered team climate data from sales staff, both pre- and post-training. After their leaders had been trained, staff reported they felt a greater sense of responsibility, better clarity on how their roles fitted with organisational goals and stronger team spirit.

Next, the research looked at impact on sales. Power motive training took place in late 1972. Sales and profit rose substantially for the business by the end of 1973. While attributing cause and effect is impossible, what was most interesting was that the geographical areas of greatest sales increases occurred in the teams where post-training climate improved.[4]

As McClelland said of the psychological foundations of motive training:

> ...it affects motive strength, probability of success, and the value placed on the particular kind of successful outcome being emphasized in the training...what is known is that power and achievement courses are effective in changing the way people think, talk and act, which in turn leads to socially desirable outcomes, such as...small business success...and more effective organizational performance from managers.[7] (p. 584)

Motive training teaches people new patterns of thought. Through this lens, change starts with an increased self-awareness of the existing patterns of thinking, which are already driving our behaviours. Otherwise, change is like trying to swim (behaviour) against the tide (thoughts).

If motives can be taught, and the power motive is most apt for leadership roles, the question arises: Which is the appropriate power stage to train?

The Power Motive and Leadership

From the 1950s to the 1990s, the 3B Institutional Leader, characterised by high power motivation, high inhibition and low affiliation, was predictive of effective performance in many large organisation leadership roles. These leaders wished to influence and have impact on others. More often than not, and more often than other motive profiles, they were able to successfully focus their team members on what needed to be done, in market context of relative stability, where rates of product and service change were relatively slow.

As David Burnham puts it:

> The Institutional Leader predictably excelled under these conditions. He (for it was rarely a she) coached others to set individual goals that were directly in line with the arousal of the Achievement motive (i.e. goals that are specific and achievable yet challenging). He was fair and just both in distributing rewards and, when necessary, in administering punishment. He provided a charismatic, inspiring vision to those he managed, and a kind of order that made the long-term direction and

future clear to all. As such, he was in a position to make decisions that he viewed as being in the best interest of accomplishing that vision. If those decisions were made fairly and within that context, no one really questioned them. In fact, employees would become upset when the leader appeared to vacillate or permit contradictory courses of action to occur. The following beliefs and attitudes surfaced in interviews conducted with Institutional Leaders: "My job is to provide answers to others." "People need me." "Everyone needs a sense of order and certainty and it is my job to provide it."[11] (p. 2)

But, as we've seen, societies changed. And those changes have huge implications for leadership and the leadership of innovation. The Burnham Rosen group is a USA Boston-based consultancy, which has carried on the work of McClelland and his researchers.

Their in-house research with clients shows that there has been a widespread shift in what accounts for superior leadership performance in large organisations. And this pattern has been seen globally and across industries. The power motive is still necessary — more so than achievement or affiliation — but stage 4 interdependent power has become much more predictive of better team climates and actual results. This is because of a mix of technological, cultural and demographic change. As Burnham writes:

> Change has accelerated — the fact that this is clichéd makes it no less true. In today's hyper-competitive business environment, expertise lasts nanoseconds before something new appears on the horizon. As a result, only well-integrated teams can effectively handle the sheer mass of information and complex problem solving. Further, although many still crave the "all-knowing, all-seeing" leader model, beware the leader who attempts to fill those shoes and then stumbles. Those who ask for "strong and decisive leadership" are the first to cry for the leader's blood! Few of the baby-boomers, later gen-Xers, and fewer still of women and minorities bring with them the assumptions of the old-style hero model of leadership (even when it is dressed up in new democratic clothing). In addition, information has become widely dispersed and readily, instantly accessible. So managers can no longer credibly plead that they alone have the information necessary to make decisions. For all these reasons, the age of the Institutional Leader is drawing to a close. Organizations that have recognized this are moving towards

structures that are more team-based, collaborative, non-hierarchical, cross-functional, and flexible. To succeed, leaders themselves must mature.[11] (p. 5)

Burnham Rosen's work focuses on power motive training and specifically, training leaders to learn to develop the power thought patterns of stage 4, interdependent power. I know about this, having been an occasional associate with them for over 10 years.

To recap on the essence of the stage 4 mode of power, leaders who conceive of power in this way, think of themselves as neither source nor target of power. They believe they derive their power from the team or organisation they lead. They think of themselves as being with others, not above them. They don't need their ego feeding, since they are not the object of their actions. They want to share information, decision-making and access to relationships in order to make others feel strong, so that, collectively, we can deal with the complexity of the challenges we face.

In a work context, as Burnham elaborated in *Inside the Mind of the World Class Leader*, the thinking of leaders strong in interdependent power affects their approach to the leadership role in the following four complementary ways:

- *Work focus*: Stage 4 leaders psychologically prepare for work by continually thinking about, planning and modifying their plans based on the outcomes that are generated. In addition, they bring a high level of pride in work. In order to do this, they work with their people to co-create meaningful purpose, capturing the essence of what will make people feel proud about their work, and attracting talented others to the work itself.
- *Mutuality*: This involves thinking of others as equals, whether or not they are above or below, in the organisational hierarchy. This involves a high degree of empathy and authenticity, as leaders consider the different skills and strengths that they and others bring.
- *Paradox and complexity*: Refers to the emotional maturity to tolerate ambiguity until the right answer emerges versus forcing things with quick, decisive (and often misinformed) action. This thinking helps people consider how to develop more flexibility to match the

paradoxes and complexity leaders face in their work. For example, appreciating that, since not all mistakes materially affect outcomes, how might we find ways to experiment with new approaches from which we can learn without generating unacceptable risks while doing so? Stage 4 leadership helps people find ways to turn ideas into action, in calmer, less impulsive, more planned ways.

- *Returning authority to others*: Stage 4 leaders think carefully about who may be the appropriate decision-maker in each situation. This is more than delegation, as it involves a process of accurately identifying who wants to be involved and who will bring ownership and pride to the work. The stage 4 interdependent leader holds the team accountable for decision-making, and does not 'jump in' to save the group if the process is 'sticky'.

This expression of power is a long way from the trust-busting, headline-grabbing 3A: personal power profile. Yet, the leaders who think in this way are thinking very deliberately about how to exercise what power they have, for the good of accomplishing shared, purposeful social goals. The stage 4 interdependent leader is very similar to that described by Jim Collins in his book, *Good To Great*.[12] When Collins describes these leaders as having high personal humility and inspiring others to follow a meaningful cause, he is talking about the stage 4 interdependent leader, but with different language.

For a more up-to-date review of this work, I talked with Rob Jackson, who is a lead trainer with Burnham Rosen, based in the UK and involved in leadership development in the UK, wider Europe and Asia. We started by discussing the big shift from stage 3B to stage 4 leadership. (Note that he often refers to stage 4 interdependent leadership as 'interactive'.)

Interview — Rob Jackson, Burnham Rosen
(RS — Rob Sheffield, RJ — Rob Jackson)

RJ: There is a fundamental shift here, because the concern is ultimately on the goal — the outcome of the organisation. It's less about the feeling of power in oneself. (Whereas with) the stage 3B leader, even though the outcomes they were seeking to accomplish were defined in terms of organisational performance, nonetheless, the psychological gain was in feeling more well-being, more powerful, a greater sense of satisfaction as those goals were met. So, in a sense, those goals were like an extension of themselves. And the fact that the leader was at the heart of those decisions, at the heart of accomplishing those, becomes a very important part of the psychological satisfaction for stage 3.

The phase to stage 4 is quite subtle, because in many respects the outcome goals are the same. People are still looking to achieve effects on customers, on consumers, or patients of the organisations. However, the psychological gain is much more away from the self. It's not about feeling powerful. It's simply about the feeling that those goals are intrinsically worthwhile in their own right. People often describe the leader as having a lot of humility. It's not so important for them to be seen to be at the heart of things. What we often see is a very strong anchoring in the actual accomplishment of work.

RS: And, to be explicit, you've been finding, with Burnham Rosen, a much clearer correlation between success in leadership roles and people possessing more stage 4 power thinking?

RJ: Yes, starting in the late 1990s and repeated studies, through to today, we're consistently finding that result…What we're finding in our studies today, is that the stage 4 leader, if anything, is becoming more predictive of the leader being successful.

RS: It seems to me that the leader might think of themselves as being something of a conduit: to make their team feel more powerful, for the sake of the work goal. They are also aware of their various sources of power and authority, but they put those in the service of the work which matters. Is that fair?

RJ: The dynamic around stage 4 is different to the dynamic of stage 3. The core of the dynamic with stage 4 is this prime concern with…a purposeful leadership. Because that's the centre of the attention: How do we accomplish these goals? In order to be effective to do that, we also see a number of other patterns of thought. One of them is recognition of their own authority but also the limitations of their authority. The effect of this is that they don't over-control. At the same time, they are looking for the establishment of accountability in their organisation. They are thinking: Who needs to decide/be involved/be accountable? The pattern of stage 3 leads the leader, at an unconscious level, to assume: it's me! The stage 4 leader let's go of that and sees the accountability in much more realistic terms. They also see others as really much more worthy of taking on responsibility. We're not all equally capable, but we bring different strengths and weaknesses. Working together, in the accomplishment of the goal, is what's important.

RS: It sounds like their thinking is around how decisions might be made that allow those who want to be engaged, to get engaged. We know that the willing engagement of others is critical to getting things done where there's any complexity or scale involved.

RJ: Yes, most leaders today will say that it's very important to engage their staff. So the question is: Why do leaders not engage their staff when they know it's a valuable thing to do? And this is the fascinating and insightful dimension that the motivational science can bring. Because, at the implicit/unconscious level, if the unconscious is not aligned to that goal of engagement, then a leader, even though they may consciously be endeavouring to empower their teams, will be sending out signals that says: 'I need to be at the heart of that decision'...It contributes to something we call 'veiled advocacy' where they describe the outcome in so much detail, that it leaves the staff member with little doubt as to what the right answer needs to be. So, in subtle behavioural ways...leaders can sometimes sabotage themselves even though they consciously know engagement is important. The value of the implicit pattern in stage 4 is that the unconscious is aligned. You have this flow between the thoughts that a leader brings to their job and what actually needs to happen for great outcomes.

RS: What do we know about how leaders learn these (stage 4) thoughts and how quickly?

RJ: In a sense it's a very simple learning process. The first phase is discovery: How do I think at the implicit (unconscious) level? The second stage is to develop confidence and a degree of comfort with introducing the stage 4 pattern. If you like, disrupting the existing narrative, and giving the brain an alternative pathway. So, instead of seeing a situation as likely to be conflict-ridden, having a low anticipation of a successful outcome, to introduce additional thinking patterns, without changing the reality of the context. Just encouraging the person to introduce additional thoughts.

The third step is having people experience those actual leadership moments in reality, hopefully experiencing a better outcome than anticipated. Then by reflecting and repeating that process, that's the process where people can make a significant shift.

There's nothing unchangeable about these implicit motives. They're simply established and habitual, largely subordinated to our unconscious. By bringing them into our consciousness and by actively working on them, we can train our brain, really quite quickly, to think about how to influence relationships in a different way.

RS: It sounds like people can make the changes pretty quickly, albeit it will be different for different people?

RJ: It's certainly our experience, yes. At an empirical level, when we've carried out robust surveys of actual change — change in behaviour and business outcomes — then we typically see that around two-thirds, sometimes as much as 75–80% of people will improve their performance as a result of developing a new pattern of thinking around influence.

RS: Given the shift to stage 4 power thinking, are there particular implications around the area of leaders enabling innovation?

RJ: Yes…there's an important pattern we've not yet talked about. And that's around people's experience of emotion. In some respects, this is one of the most fascinating and most significant insights for people going through the leadership journey of looking at motives. We know that the ways in which interactive leaders experience feelings is distinctly different from other leaders. The difference is they experience feelings in a more complex way. For example, a person may feel in one moment, frustrated, hopeful, then, in the next instance concerned and worried, but in the same minute some sense of reassurance and optimism.

This ability to experience situations in paradoxical ways — feeling 2, 3 or 4 emotions present in a situation, feelings that could be opposing, or certainly very different to each other — is a central feature of the interactive pattern. We know that this is often associated with decision-making, judgements and in particular with innovation in a work team. An important sub-element to this is, for example, how do you feel when things go 'wrong'? If you primarily experience a strong negative feeling, then, generally speaking, in psychological terms, we describe that as driving action to clear away that feeling. It can lead you to take decisions which seem at one level rational, but at another level are really trying to minimise the experience of this uncomfortable feeling. That shows up in behaviour as constraining innovation and experimentation.

When we look at groups and leaders who are particularly skilful in leading change — they typically 'code' very highly in this paradox pattern, and there seems to be something particularly important in this pattern that helps innovation.

RS: It sounds like they've given themselves more options by an ability to think in a mature and a flexible way. It gives them room to acknowledge that mistakes can be made that might not always be detrimental. Even having multiple feelings about an innovation…you can imagine how that leader might be able to find space to innovate within some boundaries that make it safer, or possible to both 'fail and succeed' — room to take action, rather than results being black and white.

RJ: One of the crucial things is the psychological tendency, under stress, to polarise decisions. To feel there's a high road or a low road. That polarisation shuts down options, and it's where a lot of innovation is lost. But it is dynamic, for example, being very attentive to the ultimate outcomes and less concerned about the process and activities ... means that a leader is more focused on outcomes, and has fewer predetermined beliefs about how it is accomplished, that creates some space.

Also, seeing oneself as not necessarily central to all decisions, that others need to take decision and others have capacity to contribute. That also increase the space for others to bring their information on to the room. Finally, having belief in others — they have different strength and abilities — that creates a more open-minded approach to relationship and their values. All of these things come together to create space for leaders, and create a slowing down of the thinking process. Better judgements get made and people are more comfortable to operate in a space of greater ambiguity.

The Leadership of Creativity and Innovation

Rob Jackson ends by describing how interdependent-minded leaders aid innovation. These leaders hold people accountable for their actions, and demand others' active involvement in the decision-making process. This form of leadership is tougher than it appears at first glance, and rewarding in learning, growth and results for those who experience it. My experience, as an educator, positional leader and team member is that more people want to be led in this way. They want their leader to be less concerned with their own ego, more focused on goals jointly agreed to be worth pursuing, calm in their collegial pursuit of those goals, and mature enough to distribute power and information.

All of which may sound a little abstract. So, how can leaders cultivate high expectations around the practice of idea development, such that it becomes embedded in team members' everyday work? When Rhodes produced his 4P framework for creativity, which we referred to in Chapter 1, he was to have an enduring impact on theory and practice. As a reminder:

Product refers to outcomes of idea development, which might be tangible products, intangible services, new brand positioning, improved customer experiences, etc.

Process indicates the stages through which people work in order to develop creative ideas. This is the knowledge technology of creative thinking tools and techniques, and of facilitation of individuals and groups as they learn to do this better.

Press means the health, poorer or better, of the work environment. This is typically called climate and it has a marked effect on the amount of discretionary effort that people choose to give to their work.

And *people* refers to the various, different characteristics of the people involved in the work. Their motives, traits, skills, experience.

Rhodes pointed to the integrative potential of the model:

> Each strand has unique identity academically, but only in unity do the four strands operate functionally.[13] (p. 307)

In the ABCD model in Figure 2.1, we've amended Rhodes' work, to account for the crucial role of the leader in enabling creativity and innovation.

In this model, leaders have a set of interconnected functions, in order to enable innovation in their teams. When viewed systemically, the four parts consolidate each other, and strengthen the impact on innovation practices and outcomes.

First, leaders must align the energies and attention of people in their team with the strategic priorities of the organisation. And, in particular, those strategic priorities that need innovation. Don't underestimate this seemingly-simple task. It takes effort and imagination for leaders to help people connect abstract organisational goals with the urgent demands of their everyday work. We look at this in detail in Chapter 3.

Next, leaders have to build the skills of themselves and their team, so that people can more deliberately cultivate a mindful approach to idea development. This is the area most associated with formal training and coaching, and we review this in Chapter 4.

Figure 2.1: The ABCD model

But training and alignment of efforts to strategy can easily be undermined if the team climate is unhealthy. Leadership is the single biggest factor affecting climate. It behoves leaders to understand how they currently impact on the work climate, and to ensure their approach creates the positive climate they want. We assess the research and practice evidence around climate in Chapter 5.

When people are skilled in creative problem solving, aligned to organisational strategies and supported in their everyday work by a self-aware leader, they will still be different to each other! They will bring different backgrounds, experiences, motives, traits and moods. Leaders have to mindfully leverage that diversity potential of their people, for better, more collaborative problem solving. We cover this in Chapter 6.

Finally, Chapter 7 broadens the view by considering the issue of sustaining creativity over time and across scale, and looking at some potential, longer-term scenarios for work and society.

References

1. ERC (2016). Available at: https://www.yourerc.com/blog/post/7-rising-trends-in-employee-training-and-development-in-2016.aspx (Accessed on 12/12/2017).
2. Frost, P. J. and Egri, C. P. (1991). "The Political Process of Innovation." *Research in Organizational Behaviour* 13: 229–295.
3. Blakeley, K. (2017). Reclaiming Our Organizations Through Collective Responsible Leadership. In: *Leadership Matters? Finding Voice, Connection and Meaning in the 21st Century*, Mabey, C. and Knights, D. (Eds.). New York: Routledge.
4. McClelland, D. (1975). *Power: The Inner Experience.* New York: Halsted Press.
5. Schultheiss, O. and Brunstein, J. (Eds.) (2010). *Implicit Motives.* Oxford: Oxford University Press.
6. Litwin, G. and Siebrecht, A. (1967). *Integrators and Entrepreneurs: Their Motivation and Effect on Management.* St Louis: Hospital Progress.
7. McClelland, D. (1985). *Human Motivation.* Cambridge: Cambridge University Press.
8. Stewart, A. (1973). *Scoring System for Stages of Psychological Development.* Cambridge: Harvard University.
9. McClelland, D. and Burnham, D. (1976). "Power is the Great Motivator." *Harvard Business Review* 54(2): 100–110.
10. McClelland, D. and Winter, D. (1971). *Motivating Economic Achievement.* Basingstoke: MacMillan.
11. Burnham, D. (2002). *Inside the Mind of the World Class Leader.* Boston: Burnham Rosen group.
12. Collins, J. C. (2001). *Good to Great.* New York City: HarperCollins.
13. Rhodes, M. (1961). "An Analysis of Creativity." *Phi, Delta, Kappan* 42: 305–310.

Chapter 3

Aligning Everyday Innovation with Strategy

> They have developed technology at a rate too fast for human psychology to keep up with, yet they still pursue advancement for advancement's sake...[1]

Organisations need to know about their reputation in society. As we saw in Chapter 1, it matters in attracting people to the work we're doing. Innovation also matters to consumers, but it's not the only consideration as they assess their experience of organisations. The 2017 'Authenticity Gap' survey by FleishmanHillard[2] looked at the distance between how brands present themselves and how consumers experience them.

> Just half of our perceptions and beliefs about a company are shaped by our expectations of its products and services. The other half is influenced by information on the company itself, its culture, how it treats its staff, its attitude to social responsibility and more. (p. 4)

This seems to reflect the growing weight placed on personal identification with organisations, whether as employee, consumer or commentator:

> The companies people chose to support — or work for — are increasingly an extension of a person's positive societal contribution and a

reflection of an individual's brand. It's no wonder that consumers expect companies to articulate their purposes, live their values, generate social good and demonstrate progress against perceived issues. Vocal purpose-driven companies are benefiting by attracting and retaining talent, generating increased loyalty from consumers and the interest of new ones. (p. 12, *ibid.*)

This chapter focuses on the role of leaders in aligning the innovation efforts of their people with desired organisational goals that serve a meaningful purpose (see Figure 3.1). It sounds a rational and simple exercise in alignment: to make the case for organisational change and ask people to help with their energies, ideas and commitment. Yet, in practice, it is done variably well. Too many leaders assume that simply telling their team that ideas are needed is enough. In the following weeks and months they wonder why the expected stream of ideas isn't materialising...

Figure 3.1: ABCD model — Align innovation efforts to strategic goals

Research Overview: Creativity and Purposeful Outcomes

In his 4P model, Rhodes called this area 'Products': an idea that, ultimately, delivers value. When Rhodes wrote his paper, new and better products were largely the focus of innovation efforts. As many economies have become more service-centred, so the focus of innovation has broadened to include other aspects of work that require innovative thinking: services, markets, business models, improved internal processes, strategies, customer experiences and so on.

Organisations and their stakeholders want to see discernible changes in these innovation outcomes. And because these different outcomes are so diffuse, the consequence is that they need ideas from many people, in many teams, within and, perhaps, beyond their organisation.

Rhodes was interested in clarifying the attributes of work completed that demonstrate creativity. He pointed to the lack of rigour in defining creative attributes — a point noted by MacKinnon:

> ...the study of creative products is the basis on which all research on creativity rests and, until this foundation is more solidly built than it is at present, all creativity research will leave something to be desired...
> In short it would appear that the explicit determination of the qualities which identify creative products has been largely neglected just because we implicitly know — or feel we know — a creative product when we see it.[3] (pp. 69–71)

So what are the qualities of creative outcomes that make them 'creative'? Through extended research, Besemer and her colleagues have identified three dimensions for assessing creative outcomes: 'novelty' — referring to newness or originality; 'resolution' — how far it solves the problem for which it was developed; 'style' examines the degree of elaboration or synthesis that creates an outcome with elegance. This last point might include aspects of product or service design.[4]

A further aspect of innovation outcomes is the degree of change desired. To what extent does the new artefact constitute a smaller, incremental shift, or something more radical major? Totterdell et al. speculate that radical innovations are more likely to meet stiffer organisational resistance unless there is a supportive climate.[5]

Rhodes imagined an investigative and retrospective approach to creativity. Starting with the outcome (product); then focusing on the persons who'd been involved in producing it; looking at how (process) they had worked in order to produce it; and, finally, broadening the study to understand the context (press) in which they had worked, that had somehow supported them in their efforts.

One of the criticisms of creativity research was that the subjects of the creative product approach were often famous artists, scientists, inventor or poets, whose work attracted interest in the process that aided it. It stretches credulity to choose Picasso, Piaget and Edison as good samples, by noting their products, inferring a generalised process of creativity and then applying this process to the rest of us. But, to repeat a message from Chapter 1: we cannot have the outcomes of innovation without understanding more about the spark of creativity.

Yet, the attention on outcomes is necessary and inevitable. Leaders in organisations want change. Most of the time they want more incremental change; sometimes they want more radical change. Sometimes they want both. Quite often, they dispute the definitions of incremental and radical, so that they're not quite sure which they want.

Finally, while what Rhodes called 'product' can be thought of as the focus of our work, it is worth stating the obvious: where creativity is needed no one knows what the outcome will be. Since some degree of novelty is needed, the people involved are necessarily pursuing the unknowable.

How do leaders establish a sense of shared excitement about the future in these conditions? Anderson and West[6] looked at the components of vision and identified the following four separate aspects:

- *Visionary nature*: The outcome must be valued by the people involved. It must be perceived to be challenging and intrinsically worthwhile, as such a combination is likely to arouse thoughts and feelings concerned with exciting, positive impact on the world, and the necessary determination to persevere over time.
- *Clarity*: The vision must be understood by the people involved in the work. Goller and Bessant describe the story of

Dr. Govindappa Venkataswamy and his Aravind Eye Care in Tamil Nadu, India. Dr. Venkataswamy was the retired head of ophthalmology at the main hospital in Madurai. He wanted to give his time and expertise to prevent cataract blindness in people in rural communities. The problem was price: the operation costs around $300, and this in a country where the average rural income is around $2/day. The vision was clear — how to make eye care affordable to people who needed it — while the process for reaching it needed exploration. They achieved the goal, developing what's called the Aravind system, at a price around $25/person and with safety standards higher than many Western hospitals.[7]

- *Attainability*: People must believe that the vision can be achieved. In the process of working together, a common approach is to adopt shorter-term goals, with a clear focus on learning. Such steps give people the conviction of making progress.
- *Sharedness*: To what extent do people across the whole team, agree with and accept the longer-term vision?

The essence of all this is that leaders must arouse hope, optimism and determination regarding the future. But how do we know if people are excited by the vision, are clear about what is desired, believe it can be achieved and share it? One way is to measure this. The vision component is one part of Anderson and West's team climate diagnostic, which can be used to measure views around vision.

Another way, that can be more ingrained in everyday practice, is to ensure that healthy social processes exist in everyday teamwork. Broadly, there are two main challenges that leaders experience in aligning innovation outcomes.

Leadership challenge 1: Agreeing an inspiring longer-term purpose

Whereas vision can be thought of as an image of a desired future state, 'purpose' asks 'why do we do this?' and 'who is this for?' These questions aim to bring a focus on work that is relatively unchanging. While there may be changes in modes of delivery, customers, and offers, over time, so goes the argument, the fundamental reasons for doing the work don't change.

The search for purpose is fundamentally one of articulating a worthwhile, enduring meaning. And part of the art of the leadership role is to craft meaning in context. As we saw in Chapter 2, leaders who are strong in the power motive, and the stage 4 interdependent expression of power, think a lot about this. They think about impact on others, impressions made, reputations created, and how all of this attracts or repels talent. More fundamentally, they think about what constitutes a shared and worthwhile purpose, to which people can commit their energies over time. They know that doing good, purposeful work brings feeling of pride to people, and that this can drive high and sustained levels of effort.

On a current UK healthcare leadership programme, commissioned by the South West Leadership Academy, the 30 participants are leaders from across the Southwest of England. They come from very different institutions: hospital trusts, charities, social enterprises, commissioning units, doctor's practices, and so on; they are clinical leaders and leaders of support functions; they range in experience and authority: from first-time frontline leaders to consultants in clinical director roles. The diversity of the group is an intentional part of the design on the part of the programme commissioners. It gives the participant access to others, who represent the richness and complexity of the whole healthcare system.

As programme tutors, we discussed our purpose. This took time, and several iterations, until we agreed on: *we co-create a safe learning climate so leaders benefit from the diverse talents available, and introduce purposeful change for better health.*

We already knew that whatever success and good reputation the programme held was partly because of our efforts as tutors, but more because of the opportunity for participants to interact with each other. Our mindset for the work was important: let's help this large group of people — who don't know each other — to feel safe quickly, so they want to disclose their own truths, take apt learning risks, help each other and make the programme a kind of learning laboratory.

Providing the best conditions for learning was an immediate type of impact. Another was that these leaders must translate their learning to their own workplaces, to improve health outcomes, either directly, or through supporting others who do this. We wanted both of these aspects to drive our efforts.

Professor Carlo Ratti is an architect, Director of the MIT Senseable City Lab and founding partner of Carlo Ratti Associati design and innovation office. We interviewed him for this book, and he describes some of his wider thinking on the opportunities for architecture:

> It is about…creating a unique interface between people and the building. This is why I would like to add a more philosophical point. Architecture has often been described as a kind of 'third skin' — in addition to our own biological one and our clothing. However, for too long it has functioned more like a corset: a rigid and uncompromising addition to our body. New digital technologies and distributed intelligence have the potential to transform it, and give form to an endlessly reconfigurable environment. In the future, we could imagine an architecture that adapts to human need, rather than the other way around — a living, tailored space that is moulded to its inhabitants' needs, characters, and desires.

As we'll see later, Professor Ratti and his team are doing novel work. The thinking here describes how future architecture might interact more closely with the needs of people. That architecture might serve people, in ways that are, so far, undefined, and which need the imagination of interested, talented people. That's an example of long-term purpose — crafting being at the heart of innovation.

Leadership challenge 2: Connecting everyday innovation needs to strategic goals

This is the rational-sounding challenge: the simple-sounding one of ensuring that people develop ideas that serve to deliver our already-agreed strategic aims. For several reasons, good practice of this is not at all widespread. The 2015 Wazoku survey, described in Chapter 1,[8] found that only 53% of managers understood their organisation's definition of innovation and its fit with wider corporate goals. Among non-managers this fell to 30%. There seems to be a shortfall of basic understanding of wider innovation needs, and how these support broader strategic goals. Think of that as disconnect number 1 — the conceptual alignment.

Disconnect number 2 is in how we align innovation needs with people's everyday work. This is more of a personal and emotional alignment. In the same Wazoku survey, 38% of frontline and middle managers said they were not responsible for innovation because it was not included in their job description. And 65% of respondents said that not enough is done to encourage employees to contribute.

When individual employees don't feel the urgency and importance to innovate, as part of their everyday work, we can be sure that they'll revert their attention to other urgencies that present themselves. Why is this lack of alignment so prevalent? In our experience, the most common reason for this is that leaders and teams simply spend insufficient time sharing and discussing these concepts.

But, of course, there are also many examples of effective practice. In Chapter 5, Jane describes how she worked with her newly formed healthcare leadership team to hold full-group meetings, of more than 70 people. During these meetings, people discussed wider strategic goals, and what that meant for the improvement ideas that were needed. They also discussed, in as concrete terms as possible, what it meant for innovation in their teams. They answered questions from the large group, as best they could, about the implications for everyday innovation. And they repeated these full-team communication sessions, until they knew they had sufficient, shared clarity.

And, knowing that current urgencies tend to devour available time, they also insisted that weekly, smaller group meetings include 25% of time to be devoted to the innovation agenda. Wazoku take this practice further by advocating that employees have specific innovation objectives included in their job descriptions, to ensure that requirements for innovation are made relevant at role level.

One of the assumptions of the above section is that strategy comes first, is knowable, and fairly fixed over time. Sometimes strategy is shifting quickly, to reflect the wider marketplace. And sometimes, ideas develop such fundamental a momentum that they transform strategy. In Chapter 7's case, Prof. Carol Jarvis describes introducing a radical change to a UK university. The programme has helped raise the focus on practice-based learning, rather than more traditional teaching, and helped embed a longer-term strategic university focus on learning through doing.

Sometimes, emerging, important work helps form strategy, which goes on to align to streams of work. The relationship is circular, not top-down and linear.

Organisations are Changing from the Outside-in and Inside-out

In a personal and engaging piece, Karl Moore shares his insights on a shift in what Millenials want from their work.[9] He reflects on his career-context conversations with more than 200 students, each year, and over the last 14 years. He argues that they have become much more interested in crafting meaning and purpose in their work. As I described in Chapter 1, Moore argues that they are loyal to pursuing such work over time, but much less so to specific employers. Moore claims that they have learnt lessons from their parents that, when the proverbial chips are down, employers tend not to share the same loyalty.

He advocates that:

> Organizations who wish to prosper will focus more time on meaning at work, have an organizational purpose and contribution which gives people a sense of satisfaction and a genuine feeling that they are making the world a better place. (*ibid.*)

The message is clear: organisations had better construct and communicate a meaningful, shared purpose, if they want to attract and retain good people. The power-motivated, interdependent leaders described in Chapter 2, think long and hard about purposeful work. They are fundamentally interested in positive impact, and in building a collective and agreed understanding of purposeful work, about which people will feel proud.

In 2013, when Mark Weinberger became CEO and Global Chairman of EY, he changed the company tagline from 'Quality in Everything We Do' to 'Building a Better Working World'. This was a very explicit change in the motives described in Chapter 2. The previous tagline was embedded in the short-term, task-focused achievement motive, which revolves around standards and improving them. As his explanation makes clear, the new tagline is much more focused on collaborative, widespread impact.

> At EY, building a better working world has always been our purpose and we are now capturing that in an explicit and concise way…In a better working world trust increases, so capital flows smoothly and investors make informed decisions. Businesses grow sustainably, employment rises, consumers spend and businesses invest in their communities. More than just growth, a better working world harnesses and develops talent in all its forms and encourages collaboration. We understand our obligation to look beyond our self-interest and engage with the world. We use our global reach and our relationships with clients, governments and other stakeholders to create positive change. We do this through who we are and what we stand for and most importantly we back it up by how we act. We help our clients, our people and our communities — one project at a time. We solve the problem in front of us and move on to the next. Over time, the whole working world works better.[10]

In motive terms, Weinberger has shifted EY's focus to stage 4, power. He is acknowledging the interdependence of global working. He is focusing on the relationships with others that build trust and collaboration over time. The focus has shifted to a people-centred state of reciprocity, aimed at influencing, and being influenced by, each other, in order to build a better working world. The underlying shift is very clear: Weinberger wants his organisation to make a long-term difference to societies, and to attract people who want the same.

References

1. Haig, M. (2013). *The Humans*. Edinburgh: Canongate Books.
2. Saunders, J. (2017). FleishmanHillard. Available at: http://cdn.fleishman-hillard.com/wp-content/uploads/meta/resource-file/2017/authenticity-gap-2017-global-executive-summary-1505147721.pdf (Accessed on 08/01/2018).
3. MacKinnon, D. W. (1975). IPAR's Contribution to the Conceptualization and Study of Creativity. In: *Perspectives in Creativity* by Getzels, I. A. and Taylor, J. W., (Eds.), pp. 60–89. Chicago: Aldine.
4. Besemer, S. P. and Treffinger, D. J. (1981). "Analysis of Creative products: Review and Synthesis." *Journal of Creative Behaviour* 15: 158–178.

5. Totterdell, P., Leach, D., Birdi, K., Clegg, C., and Wall, T. (2002). "An Investigation of the Contents and Consequences of Major Organizational Innovations." *International Journal of Innovation Management* 6(4): 343–368.
6. Andersen, N. R. and West, M. A. (1998). "Measuring Climate for Work Group Innovation: Development and Validation of the Team Climate Inventory." *Journal of Organisational Behaviour* 19: 235–258.
7. Goller, I. and Bessant, J. (2017). *Creativity for Innovation Management.* Abingdon: Routledge.
8. Hill, S. and Beswick, C. (2016). Wazoku. Available at: https://www.wazoku.com/resource/everyday-innovation-report/ (Accessed on 11/11/2017).
9. Moore, K. (2014). *Forbes.* Available at: http://www.forbes.com/sites/karlmoore/2014/10/02/millennials-work-for-purpose-not-paycheck/ (Accessed on: 01/10/2016).
10. EY (2013). Available at: http://www.ey.com/lu/en/newsroom/news-releases/news_20130702_mark-weinberger-becomes-ey-global-chairman-and-ceo (Accessed on 15/09/2016).

Chapter 4

Building the Skills for Creativity

> It is creative apperception more than anything else that makes the individual feel that life is worth living. Contrast with this as a relationship to external reality which is one of compliance, the world and its details being recognised but only as something to be fitted in with or demanding adaptation. Compliance carries with it a sense of futility for the individual and is associated with the idea that life is not worth living. In a tantalising way, many individuals have experienced just enough of creative living to recognise that for most of their time they are living uncreatively, as if caught up in the creativity of someone else, or of a machine.[1]

This chapter focuses on how to build your own and others' capabilities in developing novel and useful ideas. This section of the ABCD model is what most people associate with creativity in action. It is what they experience when they are working in groups, and attempting to develop ideas fit for the challenge confronting them.

In working with leaders who are seeking to build effective problem-solving approaches in their teams, my observations are that

- they have probably experienced some creative problem-solving tools along the way, such as brainstorming and perhaps reverse brainstorming. Most of these will be idea-generating tools;
- they may have been trained in a popular methodology, like lean, or agile working;

Figure 4.1: ABCD model — Build creative problem-solving skills

- the tools they have are limited. Few leaders have mastery of a range of tools to fit to different innovation challenges;
- few leaders have in mind an overarching problem-solving process, so these thinking tools can be used for specific purposes.

Leaders really have two roles in this regard. First, because we watch and learn from them, they have to model good creative problem solving (see Figure 4.1). But leaders have a bigger role — that of enabling effective creative problem solving in others. If you have problems that need imagination, then building the skills for creative problem solving in your team will pay off many times over. Imagine if your team was able to spot a regular stream of distant opportunities and threats; and develop solutions that spanned the range from incremental to more radical; as well as crafting implementation plans to test these solutions and learn quickly about what worked and did not; then move swiftly to decide which ideas needed further investment and spreading.

Think back to the Innovation Bind in Chapter 1, and the conditions that lead us away from novelty and back to the relative safety of the familiar. Where creative work is needed, this tension is not a recent consideration. In 1817, the poet Keats talked about:

...being in uncertainties, Mysteries, doubts, without any irritable reaching after fact & reason'.

He called this 'negative capability', and was referring to the capacity of high-achieving writers to endure the uncertainties and anxieties that are inherent with creative work.[2] While writing about the pressures that go with leadership, Simpson *et al.* claim a role for negative capability:

However, its emphasis on patient waiting and on containing the pressures evoked by uncertainty can help to create a mental and emotional space, in which a new thought may emerge that can itself become the basis for decisive action.[3] (p. 1211)

The authors describe how leaders sometimes have to act when the next steps are not clear, when teams are doing work they have not done before, and where uncertainty and ambiguity are high. These can arouse feelings of anxiety, even fear, and this immediate discomfort is commonly resolved through a series of avoidance tactics, including reverting to familiar, known territory, or simplifying options into either–or scenarios. This is an existential human option — to remove the tension by reducing the apparent complexity of the situation. It simply makes us feel better, momentarily. Though the short-term palliative comes at the cost of developing any creativity.

In the moment-to-moment experiences of leaders and teams, our capacity to bear the discomfort of the unknown, and keep exploring, is a key component for success. And while the intricate developments of ideas in the moment are mainly hidden from outside view, we already know a lot about how creative ideas might emerge.

Research Overview: The Development of Creative Problem Solving

In Chapter 1, we introduced Graham Wallas and his model of the creative process. Wallas doubted that people's thinking was based as squarely on rational thought as many others assumed at the time. He described the four stages of preparation, incubation, illumination and verification.[4]

In preparation, the person becomes familiar with the challenge at hand. They acquire skills and knowledge so as to be able to pose the right questions. Much effort may be put in here, to develop explanations of the phenomenon. The challenge is investigated in all directions, deliberately and consciously. It is likely that the explanation will not come. The problem solver may let go of conscious work on the challenge, in frustration, or temporarily or for pragmatic reasons.

Incubation is that state in which our unconscious mind continues to work at the challenge without any direct effort. While we work on other, unrelated problems, or rest, the mind continues to nudge away at the challenge, perhaps associating previously unconsidered connections. Wallas proposed that we enforce a deliberate incubation period, so that the unconscious mind starts its work on the already-understood problem.

Next, the problem solver may experience the flash of illumination or insight when the way forward becomes so much clearer. The idea has surfaced and is promising. Wallas pointed out that this phase cannot be forced or influenced by a direct effort of will. The moment of illumination is unpredictable.

Verification is the final stage. Unlike the second and third stages, it entails a more deliberate and conscious process of thought. We may test out our evolving thinking with others and incorporate their comments. We may develop experimentation to test and develop our idea. The goal is to both strengthen the idea and build agreement with powerful others.

Wallas pointed out that, in our real lives, we are likely to be working on several problems simultaneously:

> In the daily stream of thought these four different stages constantly overlap each other as we explore different problems… Even in exploring the same problem, the mind may be unconsciously incubating on one aspect of it, while it is consciously employed in preparing for or verifying another aspect.[4] (pp. 10–11)

What's clear about this process-based view of creativity is that different types of thinking state are needed, and they are all crucial:

- Conscious, deliberate thinking where we are becoming accustomed with many perspectives of the work challenge.
- Unconscious 'downtime' where the brain continues to process thoughts, without our active 'control'.
- Imaginative phases where divergent thinking is needed to explore many possibilities and withhold premature judgement.
- And an evaluative type of thinking where we select and prioritise promising, even intriguing ideas. Then we test, refine them, and share them with others for the purpose of strengthening them and securing agreement on how to proceed.

Across the Atlantic, James Webb Young reflected on the creative process from his experience as an advertising executive. He'd been invited to present his thoughts to students from the University of Chicago. He captured these thoughts in a compelling, insightful and brief book called *A Technique for Producing Ideas*, originally published in 1939, and is still in print today. Young's stages are strikingly similar to those in Wallas' model. He describes stages of gathering and digesting raw material, in relation to the challenge. Then a stage of unconscious processing, when he advocates turning imagination and emotion to whatever can occupy the mind completely. An 'A-Ha' moment, when an idea will present itself, unbidden. Finally, the idea must face the scrutiny of others. He suggests that many good ideas are lost at this stage. Young strongly advocates that we:

> Do not make the mistake of holding your idea close to your chest at this stage. Submit it to the criticism of the judicious. When you do a surprising thing will happen. You will find that a good idea has, as it were, self-expanding qualities. It stimulates those who see it to add to it. Thus possibilities in it which you have overlooked will come to light.[5] (p. 39)

Alex Osborn was a partner with the advertising agency Batten, Barton, Durstine and Osborn. He was also interested in human imagination and helping people learn to apply it. Osborn was highly influential. He wrote the book *Applied Imagination*[6] in 1953 and helped establish the Creative Education Foundation in 1954, with the aim of helping people learn creative thinking. He noticed that efforts to use a deliberate process and tools seemed to lead to better outcomes in managing change. He also concluded that such learning needed to start before we reach the workplace. With Sidney Parnes, they started work in formalising and testing an explicit creative problem-solving process at Buffalo State College (later, Buffalo State University).

Research conducted over more than 50 years researchers at Buffalo State gave academic credibility to the notion that the model, creative problem solving could be learnt. This academic research was the world's first systematic effort to understand, articulate, test and refine models of the creative problem-solving process (see Figure 4.2). It has led to a current

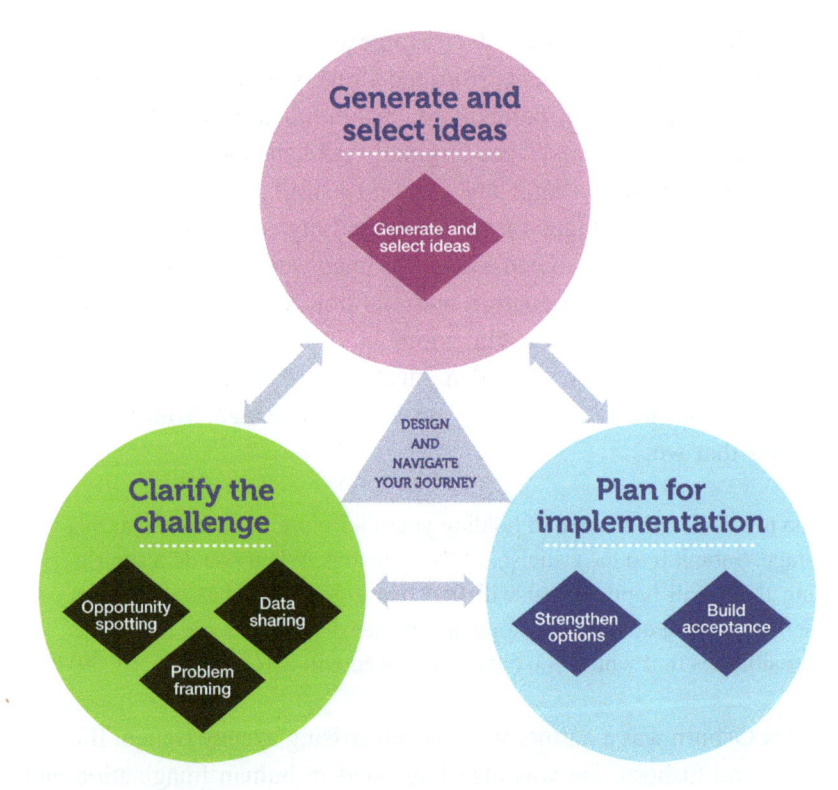

Figure 4.2: Creative problem-solving process (Adapted from work by Creative Problem Solving Group, Inc, Center for Creative Learning and Creative Education Foundation)

articulation of the model, which Wallas, Young and Osborn would all have recognised, and which adds important other features.

The term 'creative problem solving' (CPS) has eased into this chapter, and Ruth Noller gave a helpful description of the term:

> By creative we mean: having an element of newness and being relevant at least to you, the ones who create the solution. By problem we mean: any situation which presents a challenge, offers an opportunity, or is a concern to you. By solving we mean: devising ways to answer or to meet or satisfy the problem, adapting yourself to the situation or adapting the situation to yourself. Creative Problem Solving or CPS is a process, a method, a system for approaching the problem in an imaginative way resulting in effective action.[7]

Before looking at each part of the model, there are some general points to make. First, this approach is not suitable for all problem solving. It suits the type of challenges where

- the problem itself is open to interpretation, and needs clarification, definition and agreement between people who have the authority to act;
- human imagination is needed because there is no single, right solution;
- a diverse group is needed because the challenge is too complex for any individual to solve;
- the implementation of the solution will need a committed group.

The model represents an idealised form for channelling imaginative effort to the types of complex challenges that need it. It's not intended to replace all the ways we've learned of applying effective, personal problem solving. Also, other problem-solving approaches exist, such as lean and agile thinking, TRIZ and human-centred design thinking. I have chosen the Osborn–Parnes method because of its research heritage and the depth of evaluation of its practice.

Second, the model is also context sensitive. It might not be necessary for a group to work through all of the stages. Sometimes the problem might already be crystal clear and agreed. Or an intriguing solution might be partly developed and needs strengthening and 'selling' to others. Part of your leadership skill is in working out where to start.

Third, it is componential — it is intended that groups work through parts of the model at a time. Each of the three broad components take time and add value. It is not feasible to work through the whole in one sitting. It's also not desirable to do this, since time is needed to allow thoughts to 'incubate' and develop in between formal, group work.

Finally, note that each component has aspects of divergent thinking, when many options are generated, and a convergent aspect when focusing and narrowing is needed. The balance of these two — and the judgement of when to stop diverging and start converging — is at the heart of the creative process.

We describe each section of the model later in the chapter, but first, let's understand the significance of the divergent and convergent aspects.

Divergent and Convergent Thinking

In this model, the broad value of divergent thinking is in helping us generate many and varied types of options. These could be options throughout the whole process, for example, in generating many potential types of solutions to the challenge being discussed, or potential ways of reframing problem definitions. Our divergent thinking is the prime source of variety, originality, quantity and possibility in this process. Without possessing capability through divergent thinking, our solutions are unlikely to be novel.

Convergent thinking is needed to narrow down the range of options into workable, feasible 'next steps'. In practice, this can mean shortlisting, screening, sorting, refining, categorising and evaluating options, as well as using experience and judgement to plan, spot assumptions, deduce and infer. Without having capability through convergent thinking, our solutions are unlikely to be useful.

Without convergent thinking, no meaningful action is possible. We might be left with 120 potential solutions, and no route to choosing the ones to take to the next stage. But, too much convergent thinking, or done too early, may not give us enough opportunity to generate novelty and excitement.

Most people's experience of education and learning is that we are well served for help in developing our convergent thinking. But divergent thinking skills are something different and few of us have had help in learning these skills. Yet, divergent thinking has been well researched. Decades of research by J. P. Guilford and Paul Torrance have analysed the aspects of divergent thinking and identified the following four separate and complementary qualities:

1. *Fluency*: being able to produce many options, so the focus is on quantity.
2. *Flexibility*: being able to generate different categories of options, so the focus is on variety of types.
3. *Originality*: being able to produce options that are more rare, unusual, and novel, when compared to others.
4. *Elaboration*: Being able to provide greater detail on the ideas to make them more complete and expansive.

Paul Torrance developed these concepts into an operational, manually scored test, called the Torrance tests of creative thinking. These have been applied in educational settings, largely in the USA. They have been less used in workplace settings, because of their high cost and the time taken for trained administrators to process results.

This might be about to change. Sparcit is a San Francisco-based, 2013 start-up, and funded by the US National Science Foundation. They have produced a technology platform that claims to assess divergent thinking. Participants complete open-ended assessments, much like those created by Torrance. The difference is that results are received in minutes, at a fraction of the cost, with the scoring reliability being equal to that of manually trained scorers.

Recipients receive feedback structured around scores on fluency, flexibility, originality and elaboration. Scores are compared against those from other people in their growing database. Sparcit's claim is that this makes affordable the opportunities for divergent thinking assessment. I interviewed the CEO of Sparcit, Farzad Eskafi, in August 2017.

Interview: Farzad Eskafi, Sparcit

Rob: Why and how did you start the organisation?

Farzad: We started this company in 2013. We'd noticed that kids are extremely good at finding information and acquiring knowledge. But they're not good at being creative, and 'thinking outside the box'. We also noticed that schools, in general, teach a bit about knowledge gathering but not about creative thinking.

We thought that we have to start by understanding how we measure creative abilities. That's where we started looking at a variety of research, from cognitive sciences, psychology and other angles. We decided that the ideal way was to look at divergent thinking (using Guilford's and Torrance's methodology). So, we thought: How do we do this? We built an online engine around it that automates the grading process. Instead of a person leading these assessments, an engine can do it.

Rob: What interest was there in the idea?

Farzad: I talked to some 200 educators about this project and how it could be useful. They said, 'This is wonderful, but there's no funding for it'.

In the workforce, people were much more receptive for it. They told us that they have to train their people in creativity because they are not taught this in schools. So that's how the project started.

We're funded by the National Science Foundation. We took a research-based approach in building the service: making sure it's validated, reliable and that it can be used in high-stakes testing.

What we found was that, executive and middle-level leaders were most interested in our work. These people have to be creative. We're working with other talent-management organisations, to provide these creativity assessment services for both the hiring and development of leaders.

A lot of the people don't even know such a thing (getting trained in divergent thinking) is possible. Which means the sales process is longer and slower than is usual, but it's one we have to go through. At the same time, it's a clear expectation — that these leaders have to be more creative.

Our goal, over time, is to also work with others groups, such as entry-level people. But, right now, we have an educative role. It's my everyday battle.

Rob: So far, in your database, how many have completed the assessments?

Farzad: We have over 75,000 people across our total database.

Rob: And are you getting interest from some sectors more than others?

Farzad: No, it's more across the board. It's quite diverse. For example, Food, Technology and Manufacturing have all showed interest. And wider.

Rob: What patterns are you seeing in the creativity results of executives?

Farzad: Yes, this is interesting. Executives tend to score more highly on flexibility. This is not surprising: you want executives to be able to change their mindset quickly when needed. You want them to be able to look at 10 different possible solutions to be able to move forward. And that's exactly what flexibility means in creativity assessments.

Rob: Are you saying they score more highly than the general population on flexibility?

Farzad: Exactly.

Rob: And they need it, because they don't want to hitch all their 'bets' on one or two ideas?

Farzad: That, and because they may need to change their mindset quickly. In my opinion, that's even more important.

Rob: It's not helpful for them to get too attached to a certain idea. The market may tell them that they need to change their mind, or adapt it...

Farzad: Exactly. If an executive can't do that, the chances are that their organisation won't continue to exist.

Rob: It's still early in your development of this service, but do we have any impact data to show that people's scores can improve?

Farzad: We have studies on this. We have shown that, with training involved to develop people scores in between the two assessments, scores can improve over time. I think that people can be trained to become more creative. But, equally, if you don't practice it, you might become less creative over time.

Rob: And what do you know about the impact on work of improved divergent thinking?

Farzad: This is difficult for us: to get data on these examples, partly we don't always have ongoing access to the examples. But what we do have is data to show that people who score high on these assessments tend to get promoted more quickly over time. Also, they tend to save money for their organisations.

Rob: Finally, do you notice any differences in scores around originality?

Farzad: We do see a pattern, which is that roles in public relations and marketing, research and development, sports and entertainment all score higher in originality. It's probably something to do with the greater rate of change desired. Your job is to come up with new ways of doing something, all the time. It's more about radical change, less about incremental improvement.

Sparcit claims that its sophisticated artificial intelligence can identify and measure divergent thinking. The claim that machines can identify and categorise divergent thinking, faster, cheaper, and as accurately as humans is not lost here. The significance of this work is that it puts a measure of divergent thinking within the reach of many more of the population. Also, they claim that their initial dataset is promising in showing that divergent thinking capabilities can change, and over a short time period. The early results are promising, especially when testing is followed by intensive creativity training, and then retesting. This needs more widespread research.

While formal learning in divergent thinking has not been a common experience for many of us, there is a set of principles for putting divergent thinking into effect. Various studies have shown that learning the following guidelines leads to the effective application of divergent and convergent thinking skills.[8–10]

Principles for Divergent Thinking

1. Defer judgement

When you need novel thoughts, withhold judgement until later. Like the effect of a handbrake on a car, criticism is an instantly effective tool for stopping the flow of ideas. If you need the imagination of the team, and many, different, unusual ideas, this is a critical principle. The place of judgement comes later in the process, usually in the convergent stage.

2. Go for quantity

If you have one idea and are under time and workload pressures, or, if that idea has been submitted by the leader, or, simply, if it sounds good…then you're at risk. It might be tempting to stop there and you might find easy agreement among the group. But placing all your bets on one solution is probably a quick way to feel better in the moment, and a sure way to lessen your chances of success. As Nobel Laureate Linus Pauling said, 'the best way to have a good idea is to have lots of ideas'. Of course, this fits directly with idea fluency, and is also likely to help our idea flexibility.

3. Make connections

The more 'dots' there are, the more likely we are to forge interesting, unusual connections. The human brain seems well suited to this. Encourage people to build on others' ideas with their own thoughts, leading to interesting combinations. New categories of thought often emerge from this, so it can be an aid to flexibility of ideas, as well as elaborating on the detail of earlier, initial ideas.

4. Seek novelty

This principle, in particular, is about encouraging groups to spark original and unusual thoughts. The other three principles help to produce many, different, interesting ideas, but, not necessarily, novel ones. If your challenge genuinely requires breakthrough ideas, then this rule can help. Encourage people to imagine solutions outside of the current paradigm, as if it didn't currently exist. Or, if we didn't know about it. People usually have fun with this. And it can lead to surprising and exciting developments.

Some people's initial response is bodily discomfort! They shift in their seats. It all sounds, somehow, 'childish'. Given a tactful nudge and encouragement to 'just try it', they usually have a positive experience. First, they demonstrate self-control, through deferring judgement. As the ideas proliferate, so they are able to connect them in interesting ways. The process is often fun, with people building on others' ideas and being surprised with the possibilities that are emerging. There is more laughter in these sessions than most work. Some may still struggle with letting go of a known path and a known end point. But most people learn these principles quickly, and their application almost always leads to more and better ideas being generated, leaving opportunity for whittling out and developing the creative ones.

Story: The Hagrid Concept

The group of students sat facing the Professor as she described the problem. With the imminent build of a new engineering faculty building, how might the designers facilitate interactions between staff and students that meet the needs of both? Lecturers need space for teaching and research. And their availability can be a bottleneck, for busy students needing urgent information and support. This might require a change in attitudes and mindsets. The Professor invited a range of potential solutions. She wanted radical solutions to be part of their shortlist.

The group of engineering students had generated some 25 ideas, and were stuck. Their energy had slowed. One said: 'I think our ideas are not radical enough'. I chose the random object tool, and asked them to try it. I reassured them about the relevance of the tool, though the object had nothing to do with their problem!

I passed around an 8-inches tall cone-shaped spool, with a cardboard structure, and a hollow interior. Around the structure was deeply-wrapped white string, from base to top. The group of four passed it between themselves. I told them to write down their thoughts individually, not sharing them for now, so that their immediate, different thoughts of the object would be captured in all their range. For the next step, I told them to take a few minutes and connect some of their thoughts to the actual business challenge. In other words: generate potential solutions. There was some scepticism, and much laughter. Some sat back in their chairs, momentarily stumped. Then someone said, "Well, the rope provides a thick buffer...and someone else said: 'Yes, a bit like Hagrid in Harry Potter — he's a sort of gatekeeper for the students. Deals with their questions and problems. They don't have to go to the teachers...'

From this simple, novel connection the group developed a series of feasible, potentially useful elaborations. The multi-faceted 'Hagrid' concept equates to volunteer staff in the new building, helping students get where and what they needed; and a central information point; and we might 'buddy' students with students in their year above; as well as administrative staff; and the building could be partitioned, using projected, differently-coloured light, for different functions on different times and days; and lecturers might make themselves accessible at agreed times but not others...

'Hagrid' morphed into a more abstract concept of enabling mechanisms to get students source help, without the necessity for finding busy lecturers, who may not be the right people to speak to anyway. The bottleneck of lecturer accessibility could be removed. When the group presented the concept to the client-professor, she loved it.

In the learning review at the end of this session, I explained that the rationale behind the random object tool is that it forces a 'stuck' group, to think of something stimulating but unrelated. And then, to force a connection back to the real challenge. One group member asked whether the outcomes would have been different with a different object. I think he wanted some degree of predictability about the process. I said that no one could know, but that this thinking tool has been used widely, and that humans are very able at making connections between seemingly unrelated thoughts.

Having generated many and varied possibilities, the moment comes when we have enough and need to sift, sort, develop, select, cluster and shortlist options. The risk now is that the excitement, energy and sense of possibility we produced collectively through the divergent phase, will be removed, as we apply our map of the 'reality' of the organisational context. Convergent thinking is an essential part of each stage of the creative problem-solving process. And while many of us have been educated in aspects of convergent thinking, far fewer have learnt how to use them with the goal of developing ideas.

Principles for Convergent Thinking

As with divergent thinking, there are four principles that bring convergent thinking to life, which are as follows:

1. *Apply affirmative judgement* is about using critical thinking, rather than fault-finding. Essentially, point out the positives and the limitations of ideas. This even-handedness sets a tone of curiosity and retains the crucial element of possibility even as we select which ideas

to take forward. A tip: when evaluating thoughts, start with the positives, make them genuine, then list the drawbacks. Some people take feedback of their ideas as criticism of themselves, and feel it as much as hear it. Don't hold back, but do be mindful and balanced.

2. *Keep novelty alive* aims to sustain and protect the novel thoughts that emerged earlier. Remember that creative ideas are both novel and useful. *And* is the most important word in that sentence. Be mindful of remaining open to the unexpected, as well as deliberately retaining aspects of novelty that were produced earlier. As people consider their version of organisational realities — people, politics, conflicts, resources, etc. — it is tempting to whittle out novelty, and return to familiar, already-tried approaches.

3. *Check your objectives* reminds us of our aims. Earlier divergent thinking encouraged a free expression of thoughts unconstrained by real-life constraints and contingencies. Here, what matters is meeting the criteria of the organisational problem owner, and whichever interest groups are implicated in the problem: consumers, clients, etc. One risk here is that decisions are made for shortlisting options that exclude the best and alienate many of the team. Remind yourselves of the purpose of your work on this challenge. The aim is to retain earlier novelty and to combine it with usefulness, in order to help solve the problem. Such transparency with your decision-making authority will be appreciated by the people who have invested efforts and imagination in the process.

4. *Stay focused* refers to investing the time and energy you need for this stage of the work. It is quite common for teams to spend 80% of the time on divergent thinking and 20% on convergent thinking. This is a mistake. The frequent consequence of such is that ideas are poorly developed, or choices are made, in limited time available, to which people are barely committed. In this case, the limited time and energy given to convergent thinking can lead to poor decisions. What people learn is that time spent generating ideas is ultimately wasted. Such practices will undermine the goodwill of people. Give due time for people to shape, discuss, develop and reflect on ideas. People will typically go through cycles of iteration: refining, building, strengthening, connecting ideas so that what was initially proposed has been improved with due time.

Components of the Creative Problem-Solving Model

To add to the following section, a couple of explanatory points are needed. First, there are typically three types of people-role involved in the creative problem-solving process:

1. The client, who 'owns' the challenge being set, and has the authority to act on the ideas produced.
2. The resource group, whose role it is to work on the challenge set by the client. These people will work through the stages of the CPS process, aiming to develop and strengthen novel and useful ideas.
3. The facilitator, whose role it is to work with the client and resource, group. Specific aspects of their work will include co-designing a process that suits the requirements, and to choose appropriate tools for each CPS component to help the group generate and select options.

Each of these roles is mentioned in Table 4.1, along with the use of specific thinking tools. This is not a how-to-use-creative-tools book, as many of those already exist. However, please visit the resource section at the end of this book for a downloadable resource of creative thinking tools — you may find these helpful.

Table 4.1: Creative problem-solving components overview

Component	Divergent thinking	Convergent thinking
Component 1: Understanding the challenge		
• Constructing opportunities	Generate possible opportunities and challenges to consider	Focus by choosing the most promising opportunities
• Exploring data	Gather and examine many sources of data, from different points of view	Identify the most important data
• Framing problems	Generate many, varied and unusual ways to state the problem	Select, or form, a specific problem statement

(*Continued*)

Table 4.1: (Continued)

Component	Divergent thinking	Convergent thinking
Component 2: Generating ideas		
• Generating ideas	Produce many, varied and unusual ideas	Identify a shortlist of interesting, intriguing ideas with potential to solve the problem
Component 3: Preparing for action		
• Developing Solutions	Find ways to strengthen the promising ideas	Analyse, evaluate, prioritise and refine the promising solutions
• Building Acceptance	Identify sources of potential assistance and resistance	Formulate plans to gain support for, carry out, and evaluate specific actions

Source: Adapted from Ref. [14].

Component 1: Understanding the Challenge

Constructing opportunities

Sometimes, the situation may present an insight into an organisational, or market, opportunity. It is likely to be broad and ill-defined and people will make sense of the situation in different ways. The aim of working through this phase is to choose a broad, brief and beneficial opportunity to pursue. The model suggests that groups should do this through, first, generating a range of potential opportunities, and then selecting ones that resonate most with the person responsible for the eventual results — the client.

The selection of a person, or persons, to fulfil the role of client is sometimes overlooked in the planning of this work. Isaksen et al.[11] provide a pragmatic set of criteria for selecting well-suited clients. They should possess the 3Is:

- *Interest*: The client should be interested in working through a CPS process. Such work is intensive and can be time consuming. This is a matter of commitment and motivation for the client. If their energy level is high, and they are convinced about the need for the approach, this will be apparent to others. If they are distracted by other work priorities, so their limited attention will affect the people gathered to produce ideas.

- *Influence*: The client should be in a position to influence what happens with the solutions developed. When the people generating potential solutions know that the client is able to implement chosen solutions, this can only ground the process and give it a reality check. The client's influence may also be supplemented by more senior corporate sponsorship, to give added support.
- *Imagination*: To what extent does the client want novelty developed through the process? The CPS process has evolved very specifically to produce new and useful ideas. It is very helpful when the client is personally convinced that something new is required (whether more incremental or more radical). If the client already has a view on the desired solution, this will undermine the whole process. What the idea-developing group look for in the client is a genuine attitude of openness and curiosity.

Exploring data

Whatever the opportunity to be pursued, it is likely that you will already have relevant data. Find it and share it with the people about to develop solutions. Examples of 'data' will be pertinent to the opportunity selected, but could include feedback from customers, competitor behaviour, reflections on internal organisational capabilities, your intuitions and feelings, more formal survey data on, say, market trends, and questions arising from reflection on all this data. The divergent phase will likely involve sharing and generating the many separate insights and aspects of data you possess. The convergent phase will select those that seem most apposite for you, and may involve a highlighting of these seemingly key, telling data points. And, where there are data gaps, this could include the need to gather more data.

Framing problems

It is not unusual for individuals and groups to jump straight to solution generating before identifying the problem. People do this because of the perceived pressure of available time, and/or because they prefer the excitement of solution generating, and/or because they might assume the problem is obvious. It's well worth developing the discipline and ability to challenge this assumption.

Norman Maier was exploring our problem-solving approaches from the 1930s onwards. He argued that leaders should adopt an attitude of problem mindedness rather than solution mindedness. The former explores the nature of the problem situation, while the latter reflects an anxiety to reach a solution with the problem as presented. Maier argued that too great a rush to solutions is likely to block inventive thinking about possible solutions, as well as leading to their premature evaluation.[12]

This stage of the creative process involves interpreting and framing the problem or challenge at hand. The purpose of the divergent phase is to generate many potential problem statements. The convergent phase devotes time to discussing the merits of interesting ones, and to selecting one that captures the essence of the problem.

There are three broad benefits when this is done well. First, through working together to produce alternatives and discuss the merits of possible redefined problems, the group and client will come to a process of agreement. This increases the engagement of these people for the remainder of the process.

Second, as a result of the group exploring alternative, redefined problem statements, the client is very likely to select a problem that is framed differently from that initially presented. The problem chosen will resonate more strongly, and is likely to get to the root of the issue.

Third, the redefined problem statement is more likely to guide the resource group to focus on the types of ideas actually needed.

And how do we know that the problem statement chosen is, somehow, better? Isaksen *et al.*[11] list the five following attributes of a well-defined problem statement:

- *Invite ideas*! The statement acts as an open invitation for idea submitters.
- *State the issue for which you really want ideas*. Somehow, the statement captures the real challenge.
- *Are concise*. They are stated in few words — around 5–7 — and act as a starting point for solutions.
- *Locate ownership*. They state the person, people or team that has ownership for the problem.

- *Are free of criteria*. For example, it is unhelpful if problem statement asks for ideas 'that might be implemented within a month', or 'which would acceptable to the finance director', etc. imposing constraints at this stage simply acts to limit the subsequent ideas. it is better to evaluate the ideas at a later stage, than to limit them from the start.

I will add another criterion here:

- Don't embed the solution in the problem statement. For example, the question — 'How might we restructure the marketing department to ensure we understand our customers better?' — assumes that restructuring is part of the solution. It might not be, and, either way, is likely to limit responses.

The essential balancing act here is to be very focused on the problem that needs addressing, and to be open and inviting in requesting solutions to fix that problem. This real life and current example illustrate the point.

> Buildings are horribly inefficient consumers of heat...The huge atriums that many firms build as corporate status symbols, are usually occupied by no more than a handful of people, yet every cubic foot is kept warm around the clock... Professor Carlo Ratti, director of MIT's Senseable City Laboratory..., was musing on this while sitting outside a restaurant...[13]

This could be considered an opportunity. The broad, brief and beneficial goal might be framed around reducing energy waste in corporate buildings. The article continues by pointing us to various sources of relevant data, including a research paper co-written by Ratti, all of which helps to give depth to the challenge:

- 'Small wonder that building heating, ventilation, and air conditioning (HVAC) account for 13% of total energy consumption in America'.
- Commercial buildings account for nearly 20% of the US national energy consumption, or 12% of the national contribution to annual global greenhouse gas emissions.

- Ratti and his co-authors concluded, 'The results of the study demonstrate that overall the operation of the HVAC systems of the buildings, somewhat unsurprisingly, closely followed the external temperature...'
- They added that this correlation with external temperature and the HVAC system seemed more important than that between HVAC and people occupancy. Although, not surprisingly, people occupancy was quite closely associated with amount of electricity consumption.[14]

How would you frame the problem here? Remembering the principles from Isaksen *et al.* above, take a moment and write down a well-framed problem statement.

When we've presented this same problem to groups of college students or to workplace professionals, most focus on the inefficiencies of buildings; their design being ill-suited for current consumption patterns; or reducing negative impact on the environment; the attitudes of building users towards energy consumption. All of these are legitimate and potential ways of framing the problem. And all statements would have consequences for the subsequent solutions developed.

Professor Ratti took a different route, and started to wonder how we might correlate people occupancy much more closely with HVAC consumption. Though he didn't state the problem explicitly, his subsequent framing could be expressed as:

'How might... my team heat people in buildings?'

When we share this framing with students, they usually smile at the simple elegance of the problem framing. And, subsequently, the statement guides their solution generating. As we'll see later, the same was true with Professor Ratti and his team.

Component 2: Generating Ideas

In one way, this is a simpler stage. The overall goal here is to generate many, interesting, intriguing and novel potential solutions, and to reduce the many to a workable shortlist, still with those same qualities.

The starting point is a clearly defined problem that invites the imagination of people to produce many, varied and unusual ideas. Of all the stages, this has the greatest emphasis on divergent thinking.

The final, shortlisted ideas may not be fully formed and thought through. They may need development and strengthening. (That is the aim of component 3 — preparing for action.) Ideas in this stage may be quite fragile and need careful treatment.

It is crucially important to generate novelty in this section. As a rule of thumb, groups find it relatively easy to make novel ideas feasible and 'useful'. It a tougher mental challenge to add novelty to already-useful ideas.

People going through this stage often exhibit great energy. It is often fun and highly engaging. One healthcare leader described how generating ideas had produced the unexpected benefit of drawing his team together more closely. The experience is usually positive and can help make a team more coherent.

At the end of such work, people are often tired. It is an intensive and fully-absorbing work. The art of the facilitator, requiring high interpersonal sensitivity, is to judge when to push the group for further effort, and when to encourage people to take a break. High effort levels are required, along with pauses to allow for incubation, discussion, distraction, housekeeping and reflection.

Part of the research rationale for this comes from the *principle of extended effort*. Parnes[15] found that options generated earlier in idea-generation sessions tend to be more familiar and obvious. In effect, people state the solutions they are already considering. With subsequent waves of solution generation, interspersed with breaks for incubation, the options often become more original. More ideas are produced, giving people the possibility to combine ideas in more unusual ways.

As through the whole CPS process, the role of the facilitator is key. S/he will be able to call upon a wide variety of thinking tools, to suit the contextual demands of the team and the challenge. Which means they will need experience and skill in using these tools.

Part of the work of the facilitator in this stage is to encourage variety and range in individual thinking and, later, to bring together these many, individual thoughts through group discussion so that effective, novel combinations can be formed. Tools such as brainwriting are effective at encouraging individual contributions, and also provide encouragement for quieter group members.

Other tools, such as Morphological analysis and classic brainstorming, can be done individually or in groups, allowing the facilitator to optimise the breadth of ideas from individuals with the energy and combination-finding potential from groups. When the facilitator has the skill and knowledge to call upon a variety of tools, they can better serve the different demands of the resource group.

The facilitator will also plan to meet the needs of the client. Does the client want a range of potential solutions, spanning the continuum of incremental to much more radical change? Or is their preference for solutions at one end or the other?

Gryskiewicz argued that different tools can be chosen to meet the demands of the challenge at hand.[16,17] He argued that some tools will yield ideas that deal with the problem statement directly. These solutions are more likely to solve the problem by adapting and improving, while maintaining, the current structure. These are also likely to be relatively quick and easy to implement. At the other end of the change continuum, some thinking tools are more likely to yield ideas that change the structure itself. These are also likely to be more challenging for people, and to take longer to implement successfully. As well as these poles, other tools are likely to lead to intermediate degrees of change, modifying the current approach.

Through our experience with a range of generating tools, we build on Gryskiewicz's work by summarising their potential usefulness in Table 4.2. (Part of the facilitator's role is to select the tools required for the task, to meet the needs, as defined by the client.)

Having generated many, varied and original ideas, the task now is to shortlist some for further development. The importance of this convergent phase is often underestimated. Whether through time pressures, lack of foresight, or a belief that 'the difficult part is now complete', some teams fail to do this part justice. People must be allowed time to apply tools to reduce many ideas to fewer; to discuss and clarify meanings of ideas submitted by others; even to cluster initial ideas together into more viable concepts. If this part is handled poorly it builds huge frustration for those

Table 4.2: Creative problem-solving tools and their 'fit' for incremental and radical change

Tools for incremental ideas		Tools for radical ideas	
Where ideas are required to 'fit' within the existing paradigm, creating a solution that makes the current approach better.		**Where ideas are required to disrupt the current paradigm, creating a solution that makes the approach different.**	
Ideas here are more likely to be easily accepted and quicker to implement, but less likely to be 'breakthrough' ideas.		Ideas here are more likely to be 'breakthrough' ideas, radically changing the current approach. However, they may require more 'buy-in', making them slower to implement.	
Brainwriting pool	**Brainstorming**	**Analogies**	**Pictures as prompts**
Morphological Analysis	**Lotus Blossom**	**Reversal**	**Random**
		SCAMPER	**Brainstorming**
		Super heroes	**Excursion**

who've been involved in the divergent phase. The promise at the end of that session can dissipate into inaction.

The goal is to select those ideas that are most inviting, intriguing or promising, using an initial 'loose focusing'. You may not be certain that you will implement these ideas, and they will certainly invite more scrutiny and development in the next component of the process: planning for implementation. While selecting solutions, you are mindful of the need to retain sufficient novelty. There can be a tendency for perceived organisational political, financial and cultural factors to conspire to remove novel thinking, leaving remaining those solutions with which we, and others, are more familiar.

It's also worth pointing out that there is valued, human judgement involved here. As Professor Ratti said about the importance of human judgement for designers:

> We can also use online searches to increase the repertoire of inspiration. But ultimately it is still the responsibility of the designer to make

choices. Unlike in the case of basic optimization processes (a jet engine needs to optimize performance in just one dimension), computers cannot yet tell a good design from a bad one. The role of the designer remains crucial as the person who has the ultimate say. As Ernest Hemingway would have put it, she/he controls the "Bullshit detector".

Give this convergent phase proper time, and apply the four rules shown earlier in the chapter, to enable productive convergent thinking. That way, you're more likely to retain aspects of novelty and be in a position to develop novel and useful ideas.

Returning to the example from earlier in the chapter, we don't know the process that Professor Ratti and his team worked through. What we do know is that they did develop a novel approach to their problem of:

'How might…my team heat people in buildings?'

Professor Ratti describes a broad principle that was present from the start:

How can we re-establish a closer match between occupancy and energy usage? Occupancy allows new paradigms to emerge: if, starting during the Stone Age, people followed heat, what if we could make the heat follow individuals instead?

The overall approach is undeniably novel and potentially useful, and contains a multitude of more specific ideas, synchronised into an elegant whole:

At Fondazione Agnelli, we have pioneered a new technology for personalized heating and cooling — a kind of "thermal bubble" that follows individuals inside the building and allows for better comfort and a reduction of energy waste. However, heating and cooling are not the only innovative aspects of the project. Internet-of-Things sensors permeate the building and allow the monitoring of different sets of data, including occupancy levels, temperature, CO_2 concentration, and the status of meeting rooms. Based on this information, the building management system (BMS) applies responds dynamically, adjusting lighting, heating, air-conditioning, and room booking in real-time.

(Ratti goes on to describe how the solution may have further benefits.)

> Aggregated data can serve as a test bed for research on the relationship between office design and productivity. In the near future, by analyzing statistics on the building's use, it will be possible to better understand how people behave in particular space and how this in turn can affect wellbeing and creativity.

In essence, people provide the building management system with information on the temperature to which they want to be heated, personally, within the building. Smartphones allow the building to track personal locations, and overhead, infrared heaters provide a 'local warming' for that person, where they need it. Through heating people who need it, and keeping the remainder of the building heated at an appropriate ambient temperature, it may be possible to yield significant savings.

Component 3: Preparing for Implementation

Promising, intriguing and inviting ideas often need further development. The ideas themselves may need to be strengthened, and we may need the support of others to reach the point of testing, learning and refining. And, depending on results, ideas may be adopted more widely or stopped before they absorb more resources, if they have been proven to be unsuccessful. The aim of this component is to take to implementation those novel ideas that have the biggest potential for delivering value to important stakeholders.

And the challenge is make ideas 'real'. To expose ideas to use-in-context, scrutiny, feedback all in the service of improvement. Wallas called this stage 'verification' and Young referred to the 'self-expanding' quality of ideas: good ones attract interest from people, which adds to, and improves them.

As a generalisation, this is not done well in many sectors. In UK healthcare, for example, few accessible mechanisms exist for mindful learning from implementation and the wider adoption of ideas. There is a mass of employee goodwill, and no shortage of idea generating, but there is much less in the way of enabling structures to test and spread promising ideas.

Unlike the previous stage, the emphasis here is on turning ideas into action. That can mean prioritising ideas through tools like the evaluation matrix, or through comparing ideas with each other, using paired comparison analysis. It can also mean weighing up the potential strategic impact of shortlisted ideas. Checking ideas against strategic plans is a solid way of making choices at this stage.

And innovation dreams might overlook organisational realpolitik. Who might be interested in your idea, and oppose it? How might we plan, imaginatively, to build support, while minimising resistance to these ideas? The stage can also involve pitching ideas to those with resources, so they decide which ones to take further.

All of the above require both divergent and convergent thinking. But, whereas the *Generating Ideas* component needed an initial 'loose focusing', this component is different. The convergent thinking is stronger and more visible. Some ideas will be taken forward, and others, very likely, will not.

In Professor Ratti's example, the team developed a physical prototype at an office location in Turin.

> The initial idea was there from the beginning, but in order to get to the final prototype I would say that we had at least 10 design iterations… Sometimes, however, it is more difficult to convince clients. That's why tests and prototypes are very important — as they help turn an abstract idea into something tangible. We like to start with prototypes, and then see how they could be adapted to the real world. This is the path we always follow in innovation. Every time you need to start again from scratch — but you have learnt something from the previous iterations.

As he describes, the team went through successive design iterations, learning and refining, and treating this process as an essential part of the creative process. When we last corresponded in Autumn 2017, I asked for an estimate of the potential benefit of the idea:

> It is too early to say, considering that the building was opened only four months ago during the summer. However, we still stick to the idea that

potentially we could slash energy consumption by up to 40%, especially in sparsely occupied spaces.

Ten Practical Implications for Leaders

In working with organisational leaders across different hierarchical levels, we have found that they and their team members learn the method quickly. It is a reliable way of building human capabilities that can be repeated again and again. However, it is not 'foolproof', and doesn't guarantee 'success' in every situation. The following are some important implications for leaders:

1. *Become a better pilot.* Learn to navigate your way through the CPS process. You may not need all of it, every time. For example, sometimes, the idea brought to you is already good enough to take to stage 3: preparing for implementation. Or, equally frequently, an idea seems to have no discernible problem to solve, but is beloved by the idea holder! Develop your diagnostic and navigation skills, so you and the team take the next step needed.
2. *Separate divergent from convergent thinking.* Do this, not as a rule for rule's sake, but with your best judgement of how to make progress on the problem.
3. *Be problem minded.* You will need to explore, agree and define a focus on the challenge at hand. This seems an obvious thing to say, yet it isn't done as often, or well, as needed. Under time pressures, and with vaguely shared presumptions of shared understanding, teams often move onto developing solutions. Only to find later that they have, indeed, been working on different or multi-faceted problems that needed clarification. Take the time to imaginatively explore and select the best-fitting problem for your needs.
4. *Design for incubation time.* In reality, a CPS campaign might be part of a team's ongoing work, applied to a locally owned challenge. Or as part of a new products and services project, bringing people together from across the organisation. We have worked with teams that have designed part of a CPS process to last a week, and others where it is spread over months. The resource of time available is not the only

consideration in the design planning. Build in deliberate time for incubation.

5. *Provide a buffer around your team.* Part of your leadership role is to provide place, space and time to encourage people to think in this way. Temporarily remove the burden of time and stakeholder pressures. Protect your team from the too-early scrutiny of powerful stakeholders, and secure the political and resource support you need.
6. *Anxiety prefers to limit.* Be watchful of the tendency for people to polarise choices and create dilemmas. This, or that, idea? Lower cost or raise morale? Develop new markets or refine current ones? Sometimes these choices are appropriate, but, sometimes, when people venture into new territory, the polarising is an anxiety-reducing psychological strategy. It serves the immediate needs of the person, through reducing the complexity of the moment into a neat, though illusory, choice. Ask yourself whether the choice is meeting the needs of your problem-owning client.
7. *There can be a social payoff.* CPS is not commonplace for many in our workforce. It can be liberating, fun, and have the side-effect of enhancing work relationships between people, as well as making task progress. It is a new way of working for many people, one that they remember with positive thoughts. And they usually want more.
8. *See things through.* Make sure that the problem selected really matters to your team. Add determination and perseverance to the mix, so that ideas reach implementation and that you learn from the results. Point to successes delivered and aim to build a virtuous spiral of capability building and positive results.
9. *Be fair.* As leader, you may have a preference for a particular idea. If you do, the team already knows it. Ask yourself whether the reaction to your preferred idea would be the same if it came from another team member.
10. *Be a developer.* You may be best placed to facilitate the team through the CPS process. And you may not. Weigh up the pros and cons of giving this role to someone else, so that you can help your team in a different way. (Read the section on adaption-innovation in Chapter 6, to understand more about your and others' problem-solving styles. Your main role is to develop the CPS capabilities of your team.)

Case 1: The Ambulance Service

The context

Neil is the clinical development officer for a United Kingdom regional ambulance service. This involves discussing strategic direction with work commissioners, and being a link between them and delivery staff. Part of Neil's work is to interpret the changes needed and work with others to implement new ways of working.

A team of us from UWE Business School, had worked with Neil and others on a leadership programme, commissioned by the South West Leadership Academy. This is a team based within the UK's National Health Service and responsible for regional leadership development.

In the example below, he describes an opportunity that emerged, due to the team's move from paper to electronic care records.

The Interview

Neil: We'd noticed that we needed an update of the information we gave to patients. For example, if someone had fallen over and bumped their head, been seen by a paramedic and they were fine to be discharged. I thought this was a perfect opportunity to get the patients and staff to look at the information they need, and make sure it was fit for purpose.

Rob: What had you learnt previously?

Neil: On LIFT, (a leadership programme, run by the South West Leadership Academy), we learnt about idea generation through tools like brainstorming and reversal. That fitted in well with how I think. It's all about collaboration, internally as a team, and with external stakeholders.

Rob: And what did you do with the group when you met?

Neil: So, I formed a patient focus group of about 12 reps. I explained what we were trying to achieve. We asked them what information they'd want in the leaflet, and how they wanted to receive it — whether by email, paper based, or whatever.

We started with brainstorming to generate ideas about what a leaflet could be like for patients, when we'd discharged them at home. I brought lots of post-its and some sharpie pens.

Rob: How receptive were they to this way of working?

Neil: They were really receptive! They were pleased to be involved, and they felt proud to inform the process. Because some hadn't been involved in this sort of thing before, there was a minority who couldn't quite see what we were trying to achieve, and seemed to come along with their own agenda. They wanted to open up the conversation onto other NHS topics.

I told them: If something happened to one of your loved ones, what would you want to know? I gave them the categories: What would you want in the leaflet and how would you want to receive it?

The overall process was interesting. I joked with them to try and get a lighter mood in the room. I said to them that we don't just want my view on this.

I did think in advance about using the superheroes tool. But when I arrived in the room, I decided to start with something more simple and well known — brainstorming — so as not to alienate anybody.

Rob: How much did you find that the patient group stuck to the principle of separating generating from evaluating?

Neil: I split them into four small groups. Partly because I didn't want a large group being taken over by a strong minority. It worked well, I went around the room asking them how it was going, and encouraging them to get many ideas out now, and we'd discuss them later. Two groups bought into it well and produced lots of ideas. The other two groups were more interested in talking through their ideas as they went along. They only produced around 5–10 ideas. So, it varied.

Rob: Looking back on it, as an exercise, how happy overall were you with the quantity and quality of ideas they generated?

Neil: We had some wonderful idea generation. They came up with lots of things. We included provision for people who can't see, read or hear. So, using larger font and braille, for example.

As well as the patient group, I also got ideas from our internal quality management team within the ambulance service, and from people in an acute hospital trust. All of these ideas were put into a spreadsheet.

I was definitely happy with the quantity. Quality is a bit harder to judge. There was duplication of ideas, which told me: these ideas are something you should pay attention to. I tried to counter any conformity within a particular group by asking three separate groups, and that produced more variety.

Rob: At the end of it, how novel were the ideas?

Neil: I felt the more innovative ideas came from the quality group, who were focused on patient safety and the patient experience. They were able to simplify and streamline the leaflet, but not affect the quality.

Rob: And where are you at now, in implementing the changes?

Neil: We're talking with our design team about it and it's being reviewed by our clinical director.

Case 2: The Drug and Alcohol Dependency Team

The context

In summer 2016, I worked with Liam and his team of drug and alcohol dependency advisors. The work included introducing them to the three stages of the CPS process, and a series of thinking tools for each stage.

Liam and his team work at a large NHS organisation in the South of England. Since our work together finished, they have won a contract to extend the range of their services across their whole county. This is a big change, as their work previously focused on one large city within that county. They will now be serving 800 people instead of 250.

This is a significant success, and a reflection of the team's work. It will also bring real challenges to the team. The contract will bring more money, and a bigger team, to deliver these services. But there will be less money available for each service user helped.

Also, there's been a recent government shift in ideology. The (New) Drug strategy 2017 recognises the success of national approaches previously focused on the recovery agenda. But it also notes the specific challenges of dealing with new patterns of drug use and an ageing cohort of opiate users presenting with increasingly complex health problems.

People with drug and alcohol dependency problems go through different stages of support. First, they are assessed by a medical doctor who issues a prescription that allows a pharmacist to dispense opioids to alleviate symptoms of withdrawal. As the patient progresses through the treatment pathway, so pharmaceutical and psycho-social interventions are used in combination to support the person so they sustain their recovery.

Then they enter a clinical stage of treatment to reduce their immediate dependency needs. Finally, they transfer to a longer-term stage of recovery, with less emphasis on medical treatment and more on psycho-social support, to sustain their new habits over time.

As Liam describes it, the last 5–6 years have been 'recovery' oriented — getting people through the initial treatment and out into the stage of recovery. This contributed to a range of treatment offerings being developed:

> The recovery system we've run has been really successful — but there have also been more people dropping out of treatment for a variety of reasons. So we're trying to find the middle ground. Moving forward we will be putting more emphasis on trying to retain these people within the treatment service.

For Liam's team, the pressure is to retain more people through the treatment phase, and out into recovery. And to do so with more service users, but less resource, per person. The increased geographic scale of the work has required a review of the whole service offering.

The Interview

Rob: Back to creative thinking, how did you work your way through this?

Liam: The first thing we did was use brainstorming in our team. We got a big white board and we worked our way through identifying the different challenges: the evidence base of best practice, resources, venues, staff time, staff numbers, how many service users in each different area, local demographics, the new government agenda... There were lots of challenges!

Rob: Having listed and agreed the challenges, what did you do next?

Liam: We focused on what was in our control and we generated ideas for each of these. Again, we used brainstorming. People seem to really like brainstorming — it suits us. Because it's a such a diverse team — everyone is from different professional and personal backgrounds — we had a really good mix of ideas. At the end, there were at least nine key themes, and these branched out into more detail for each.

Rob: After that, did you go through a focusing stage to select ideas?

Liam: Yes, we did. We ran another session, and invited our psychologist along, to get her input. We used voting. The social workers from one angle, the nurses from another; the social approach, the medical approach. And we discussed our thoughts as we went along. People's life experiences are really important. We have people who are part of our own team and have been in recovery for 10–20 years.

Rob: What happened next?

Liam: We ran another session, with our medical director. We got his assurance on what we'd done. We did some more brainstorming and voting and got into more detail, looking at each part and how it was going to work in practice.

Right now, I'd say we're almost at the first full draft. Once we've got that, I'll write it up and take it for feedback to the team, service users and to partnership agencies.

Rob: So, it sounds like you've gone through these sequences to develop ideas, with different people for different perspectives, but also to get their buy in?

Liam: Definitely.

Rob: When we did our work together, did you learn anything about how to handle such a diverse team?

Liam: I realised that I was already doing it, but through the training I was taking a step back, and learn the theory behind it, to understand why I was doing it. I was doing a lot of reflection.

Rob: Give the scale of your challenge, how much has this process you've described helped you come up with novel ways of doing things?

Liam: Oh massively. When we won the contract it was brilliant. Everyone was happy about it. Then it dawned on us: this is quite scary! By working through it like this, it reassured people — especially the medical staff. For some of our users, we may only be seeing them monthly, or every two, or three months... I could see it was really reassuring for them, knowing this is really safe, and working through all those concerns with them.

Rob: Having gone through this process, is there anything new and different about the service you're planning?

Liam: There are new things — lots of partnership working, and on a bigger scale. Even though the staff will be working for different companies, it'll be one coherent, integrated service. In our immediate team, we may only be seeing people every few months, but our wider partners will see them every two weeks.

We're all reassured that the staff are all under the same service which will now be able to offer more treatment options and greater choice for the individuals accessing the service. For example, the service will be offering high, medium and low intensity psycho-social input. It allows individuals to pick a treatment pathway that benefits them more effectively.

The new integrated treatment system will also bring together existing partnership agencies, improving communication, ease of access to treatment and greater choice for service users. Integrated treatment is associated with improved outcomes of reduced substance abuse, improved psychiatric symptoms, decreased hospitalisation, increased housing stability, fewer arrests and improved quality of life.

Rob: And, therefore, having partners involved in designing and approving the process is important.

Liam: Yes, for designing the governance process, and things like that.

Rob: As a way of working — with divergent, then convergent thinking — what benefits does it bring to you and the team?

Liam: The first thing to me is the buy-in from my team and our partnership agencies. I suppose that the senior management teams could have gone away and done it ourselves. Then I'd have come back to my team and said 'This is it…'. But it just wouldn't work — it would devalue the skills the team bring, and we'd miss ideas from them.

Case 3: The Creative-writing Workshop

The context

Shelley Harris is a novelist and teacher of creative writing, as well as being a lifelong friend. I had previously talked her through how we use idea generation tools in organisational settings. She then thought about how to contextualise these for writers who attend her various creative-writing courses and workshops.

The example below includes her description of combining two idea generation tools in an unusual way. She calls one tool 'petals', and this is more commonly called 'Lotus Blossom'. She initiates the exercise by choosing a random word, to provoke the whole process, and then she helps people quickly generate more associations, from this initial random stimulus.

As a whole, what's she's describing is a type of force-fitting. In such a process, stimuli from phenomena completely unrelated to the problem are considered and examined. And then, an attempt is made to 'force-fit' and connect any insights back to the genuine problem, with the aim of enabling a next move. Force-fitting exercises like this are designed for when people are 'stuck' and/or need ideas that are original, and different to what they've produced so far.

Alice Broadway was a student on the course. She describes her experience of learning and applying the thinking tool to a specific challenge she was facing, as she was writing her book *Ink*.

Shelley's account

I learnt about the 'Petals' problem-solving technique in a conversation with you about the ways in which creativity, which we often think of it as resulting from a sort of divine inspiration, can actually be taught in very practical ways. This has particular relevance to writing, I think. It's common for people — including beginning writers — to believe that you have to wait passively for some sort of quasi-spiritual communication; a common question I get about my own work is: 'Do you just sit there and wait for inspiration?', which authors find a quite hilarious question, because in fact we really *work it* — we're grafters.

Writing is often about problem-solving — how does that character end up knowing how to pick a lock? How do I get her from Bolivia to Moscow? — and when you told me about 'Petals' I knew it would be a great way to tackle issues like that. In particular, I could see it enabled writers to side-step their conscious mind, and allow their unconscious to throw up some answers. I've found it to be incredibly effective, and now teach it in a variety of contexts. Specifically:

I've taught it on residential retreats within the context of 'moving your writing on' from where writers are. Group sizes tend to be about 6–16. I've also taught it as part of a workshop on 'Taking Risks in Your Writing', with the aim of 'reaching the parts' that more conventional approaches may not be reaching. I've done this for students in a 10-week evening class (who might number 16–18), and at writing festivals and for writing groups in one-off sessions, which might be as large as a lecture theatre of 50 or as small as a group of 8.

Alice Broadway was a student on a residential writing retreat, and I presented the exercise to the group as a way of solving a specific problem they might have with their work in progress.

'Petals' sounds a bit 'hocus pocus' when you first present it. I'm really not one of those candles-and-bells creative writing teachers; I'm mainly about pragmatism and slog. So, I present it to students by saying: 'this is going to sound like fairy dust — very weird — but it's brilliant. Will you trust me, and give it a go?'

I don't see myself as having power when I teach, but I may have authority and influence stemming from my own record as an author (I have published two novels with a major publisher, have enjoyed healthy sales and critical praise) and as an experienced teacher, some of whose students have gone on to be published themselves. The techniques I teach are things I've used in my own writing, so I tend to present in quite a collegiate way. My approach is: 'I've used this technique, and it's oddly brilliant. Shall we have a go and assess its usefulness?' In this spirit, I almost always do the exercise at the same time as the students.

When I taught Alice's group (a very small one — I think there were five of us in total) I invited them to bring to mind a writing problem they needed to solve, and we took a random word from the dictionary (one person giving me a page number, another an entry number for that page). They wrote that word in the centre of their flower and then — very fast, before they could censor themselves — they free-associated a connected word on each petal. Then I got them to look at each new word and ask themselves: 'how might this be suggesting an answer to my problem?'

I always find this an incredible exercise — it seems to bust through blocks. It's not uncommon for it to solve a problem that's been dogging a writer for months, and I think its success lies in the way it forces nonlinear thinking, prompting intellectual leaps. In Alice's group, the response was very typical, in that all the writers said they could see a way through. For one or two it had raised interesting possibilities, and for a couple it was a bit more of an epiphany.

The exercise, and the principle underpinning it, that we don't have to wait passively for inspiration, that we can create a channel for it — is one I return to again and again as a creative writing teacher.

Alice's account

When Shelley showed us, we used petals and a random word from the dictionary. I've since used it for specific questions or stuck points in my work. It enables me to get out of the nitty gritty and panicky feeling of not knowing what is coming next or how to fix a plot problem — it loosens up my thinking and lets my imagination play alongside the logical 'I need a specific thing to fix this plot hole' thinking.

For *Ink*, I knew I needed a backstory for the main character's father and nothing I was thinking of felt natural — it was obvious I was grabbing at straws and it would have read that way. I wrote a question, like 'where has her dad come from?' and found a random word and began associating words and ideas with both the word and the problem at hand.

It helped not to think so much about the problem and 'fixing' it, but just about what ideas came to the top of the boiling pot, if that makes sense? Following a series of thoughts and ideas it was clear that the answer lay in a forest. This fits nicely with the kind of writing I do — the themes that always creep in no matter what, and with the rest of the book as a whole. It also gave me a lot of new things to play with.

The ideas that came from the activity have been crucial in the final story and the second book in the series is mainly based in the forest. I get quite anxious and fraught when I'm stuck — this process loosened it all up and brought ideas that were there but hadn't been given any space to emerge.

Thanks so much for this — and for the tool, it has helped me many times! I'm very grateful!

Chapter Review: Key Learning from Building CPS Skills

In different ways, the above three cases illustrate what we've found repeatedly in helping leaders learn these skills. When they apply specific tools to real work with their team, they think hard about how to use them. They match their choices to both the needs of the people involved, and of the specific work requirements.

As a general observation, they quickly become adept at facilitating groups to produce many ideas (fluency). They sometimes have to give more thought to flexibility of ideas, to ensure different idea types. And originality of ideas often takes more practice. Idea elaboration tends to emerge in the middle, or later stages, of idea development, when people alight on ideas they like, connect different thoughts in unusual ways, and start to develop them spontaneously.

In real-life situations, effective, learning leaders also realise that it is not enough to follow slavishly the rules and processes for creative-problem solving. They learn the rationale for those rules. But their enactment comes with real people in real time and needs judgement. To use these thinking tools effectively requires a high degree of emotional intelligence. For example, without sufficient trust or psychological safety, the presence of diversity in a group remains latent — people simply don't share their thoughts, and certainly not their more original ones. Effective facilitators accurately note the group's energy levels, and take appropriate action: another 'push' for ideas, a different tool, time to incubate...

In the case above, Shelley took the risk of doing something different. But she also positioned the forced-fitting tool as being useful when writers are 'stuck', and need a thought from a different place. Neil gives examples of responding to the energy and expectations of the group, and choosing tools accordingly. Liam is working with an established team, while entering a new context, and knowing that he needs the genuine commitment of his people.

The interdependent-minded leader is helped with the challenges described in this chapter, because of their way of thinking. They already want to channel collective energies on purposeful work, in order to have a worthwhile impact on people's lives. This makes them consider carefully what is the 'real' problem.

They also want to engage people very deliberately in the process and outcomes of the work. CPS is an unusually democratic process, and group decision-making is built explicitly into the design. Interdependent leaders consider how to return decision-making authority to others, because doing so raises commitment to action and eventual impact.

Leaders who think in this way also tend to view change with a complexity of feelings. They are typically self-aware, and aware of their impact on others. When the problem needs novelty, they are likely to realise that a 'rush to resolution' may be meeting individual's needs to reduce their anxiety levels, rather than the true needs of the work. Because of this awareness, they often possess more of a capacity for tolerating uncertainty and ambiguity, which helps them remain calm, and transmit this to the group, helping the group explore for longer.

And finally, they will be highly aware of the need for diversity in the work. They think from the view of mutuality: bringing their own talents, and needing different perspectives from others. As Professor Ratti shared:

> I like omni-disciplinary approaches, where a team of people with diverse backgrounds can debate ideas and let them emerge freely. This is the reason why at MIT Senseable City Lab we have over 50 people, coming from all over the world, who speak the language of designers, planners, architects, engineers, biologists, physicists, and social scientists. "Diversity" is one of our greatest assets, and it helps us to expand our comfort zone. I think that "diversity" is becoming increasingly crucial today.

References

1. Winnicott, D. W. (1971). *Playing and Reality.* London: Routledge.
2. Keats, J. (1970). *The Letters of John Keats: A Selection* by Gittings, R. (Ed.). Oxford: Oxford University Press.
3. Simpson, P., French, R., and Harvey, C. E. (2002). "Leadership and Negative Capability." *Human Relations* 55(10): 1209–1226.
4. Wallas, G. (1926). *The Art of Thought.* New York: Franklin Watts.
5. Young, J. W. (2003). *A Technique for Producing Ideas.* New York: MacGraw Hill.
6. Osborn, A. F. (1953). *Applied Imagination: Principles and Procedures for Creative Thinking.* New York: Scribner.
7. Noller, R. (1979). *Scratching the Surface of Creative Problem Solving: A Bird's Eye View of CPS*, pp. 4–5. Buffalo, NY: DOK.
8. Isaksen, S. G. and Treffinger, D. J. (1985). *Creative Problem Solving: The Basic Course.* Buffalo, NY: Bearly Limited.

9. Millar, B. et al. (2001). *Creativity Unbound*, 3rd edition. Evanston, IL: Thinc Communications.
10. Osborn, A. F. (1963). *Applied Imagination: Principles and Procedures of Creative Problem Solving*, 3rd edition. New York: Scribner.
11. Isaksen, S. G., Dorval, B. D., and Treffinger, D. J. (2011). *Creative Approaches to Problem Solving: A Framework for Innovation and Change.* 3rd edition. Thousand Oaks, CA: Sage.
12. Maier, N. R. F. (1958). *The Appraisal Interview: Objectives, Methods and Skills.* New York: John Wiley and Sons.
13. Babbage (2015). *The Economist.* Available at: https://www.economist.com/blogs/babbage/2014/06/energy-efficiency (Accessed on 15/09/2015).
14. Martani, C. et al. (2012). "Studying the Dynamic Relationship between Building Occupancy and Energy Consumption." *Energy and Buildings* 47 (2012): 584–591.
15. Parnes, S. J. (1961). "Effects of Extended Effort in Creative Problem Solving." *Journal of Educational Psychology* 52: 117–122.
16. Gryskiewicz, S. (1980). A study of creative problem techniques in group settings. Unpublished doctoral dissertation. University of London, UK.
17. Gryskiewicz, S. (1987). Predictable Creativity. In: *Frontiers of Creativity Research: Beyond the Basics* by Isaksen, S. G. (Ed.), pp. 305–313. Buffalo, NY: Bearly.

Chapter 5

Work Context — A Healthy Climate for Innovation

> The staff restricted their conversation to service matters; they spoke to each other with a careful and reserved politeness. At meals in the legation canteen, when conversation was unavoidable, they stuck to the stock phrases of official terminology, which, in the familiar atmosphere, appeared grotesque and rather uneasy... Often it happened that somebody protested against a supposed false interpretation of what he had just said, and called his neighbour to witness, with precipitate exclamations of 'I did not say that' or 'that is not what I meant'. The whole thing gave Rubashov the impression of a queer and ceremonious marionette-play with figures, on wires, each playing their set piece.[1]

In Koestler's fictionalised account of the working of a totalitarian party, his characters are sitting together at a meal, just before opposition trials are due to take place. Adherence to Party ideology is paramount, and a clashing opinion might have dire consequences. Many of us have worked in teams where it was risky to speak too plainly. The consequences were not as severe as they might have been for Koestler's characters, but they would have affected our willingness to take a risk and develop ideas.

As Accenture describe it, reflecting on their 2012 survey with 519 companies across the USA, UK and France:

> Innovation can be a company's most powerful tool and a key driver of value. Yet many executives, fearful of the risks inherent in pursuing edgy

new ideas that may not succeed, hesitate to unleash its full potential. They prefer, indeed, to renovate rather than to innovate.[2]

Of the 519 companies in the survey, 64% are focusing on extensions of current offerings. Only 20% view their innovation efforts as potential game changers. The survey authors reason that large organisations tend to be cautious because they've developed a series of internal controls, designed to minimise risk taking, and protect stakeholders' interests. One of these controls is the stage-gate innovation process. Here, products and services move through a series of stop or proceed decision-making stages, designed to support promising ideas, and to stop likely failures early before they absorb too much resource. The process can bring a useful discipline and shared agreement. But it too often brings extreme caution through the tough evaluation criteria used at each decision-making stage. Without ever intending to do so, organisations tend to remove the groundbreaking ideas, leaving the more incremental-focused ideas to proceed. Incrementalism can seem an overwhelmingly logical and sane path, but, the authors argue, it usually does little more than maintain market share, and it can lead to slow stagnation.

The context in which ideas are developed clearly matters. If one asks the question: Where do you have most of your ideas? Most people will say something like: in the shower…the car…after sleeping…while running… What people are referring to is the moment of idea illumination, often after a period of incubation, which itself followed a prior immersion in the problem. Only a minority of people will answer 'at work'. For many, the workplace is a source of high pace and workload, with too little time and space for pause and reflection.

Ideas do not develop in a vacuum. We work in contexts, and we very rapidly absorb the social, psychological and emotional expectations of our workplaces. We may belong to a myriad of teams and different contexts in our organisations, and they all matter. Because it is through our experiences of work life, enacted in these specific contexts that we judge how seriously are our organisations' intentions towards creativity and innovation.

This perception of our 'fit' with their work environment, and the extent to which it supports or hinders idea development, is captured in the

Figure 5.1: ABCD model — Create the work climate for idea development

concept of climate for innovation (see Figure 5.1). As we'll see, it matters because climate gets at the issue of goodwill. You may have trained your people in the tools and process thinking described in Chapter 4, but if people perceive the local work climate to be too risk-averse, or even punitive, they'll probably withhold their new-found skills.

Research Overview: How Climate Affects Innovation Performance

An overview of climate

As the focus of creativity research expanded beyond the traits of individuals, to encompass the work context, so developed the concept of Creative Climate, or Press as it was initially called. 'Press' comes from the latin word *pressus*, meaning box or container. Press was the word used to describe where creativity took place, referring to the interaction between people and their environment. What are the characteristics of organisational environments that support and/or hinder creativity and innovation? That is a fundamental question legitimised by the study of Press, or Climate, as it became known.

Some clarity of terminology is needed, as much academic literature describes work climates and cultures interchangeably. Isaksen describes climate as involving:

> ...recurring and observable patterns of behavior that characterize life within the organization or team — it's what people experience. Culture is defined as values, beliefs, and traditions, reflecting the deeper foundations of the organizations — it's what the organization values. In this way, culture is treated as an antecedent to climate.[3] (pp. 131–132)

Whereas culture is composed of harder to shift, ideological foundations. Isaksen makes the strong point that, since climate is based on patterns of behaviour, and is more directly observable, it is more amenable to deliberate change efforts.

Research into climate for innovation identified a number of key variables. The nature of the work itself matters. Puccio et al.[4] argue that creative thinking is required when the problem or challenge is heuristic, that is, open ended, with no set method to follow or obvious solution. In summarising several studies, Byrne et al. build on this,[5] stating that the task must present complex, ill-defined problems where successful performance depends on the generation of novel, useful solutions.

This has implications for the design of the work organisation. The task should reflect a whole piece of work, so that people understand why it matters, as well as working on enough of the whole process, to see ideas develop in progress. There should be freedom in deciding how and when to do the work, as well as performance feedback that highlights new ways of working.[6]

Claxton argues that when people perceive there to be an environment of threat and evaluation, these impact negatively on memory, planning and creativity. People become 'tunnel-visioned' and fall back on familiar thinking. Conversely, we are more able to generate new and useful ideas when we are free from pressure and feeling positive.[7]

All of which suggests that when groups are working together, there needs to be sufficient trust between people, or, at the least, enough psychological safety, to venture together into unknown territory.

Humour and playfulness has been identified as a factor in enabling creativity. Think of this as the spontaneity and ease that exists in the workplace, reducing people's levels of inhibition — the opposite of Koestler's characters in the quote at the start of the chapter. More broadly in the realm of positive emotions, creativity can be facilitated by a transient pleasant, affective state:

> ...good feelings tend to increase the tendency to combine material in new ways and to see the relatedness between different stimuli.[8] (p. 1130)

People who are feeling happy seem to be able to access a greater amount of cognitive stimuli. The thinking is that, since creativity can be considered to involve the ability to combine stimuli in different ways and to see connections between different stimuli, positive feelings allow individuals to defocus attention and to make a greater number of novel interpretations. In other words, a happy, relaxed state aids the divergent thinking process that we described in Chapter 4.

Most case studies are retrospective write-ups of what happened, often missing the telling detail of the moments in which ideas are initiated, stagnated or surged forward. Teresa Amabile and her colleagues wanted to obtain more in-the-moment insights. They looked at nearly 12,000 daily diary entries from 238 knowledge workers, working on creative tasks in the consumer products, high-tech and chemical products sectors. In the research, participant coded their entries for the emotions they were feeling on particular days: fear, anxiety, sadness, anger, joy and love. Their results showed that people were happiest when they'd developed a creative idea. Also, their prior day's happiness was an even stronger predictor of having a breakthrough idea on the following day:

> There's a kind of virtuous cycle. When people are excited about their work, there's a better chance that they'll make a cognitive association that incubates overnight and shows up as a creative idea the next day. One day's happiness often predicts the next day's creativity.[9]

What they found about the role of time pressures was important:

> ...the participants in our study generally perceived themselves as being more creative when time pressure was high. Sadly, their diaries gave the lie to those self-assessments. There was clearly less and less creative thinking in evidence as time pressure increased.[9]

Not only was time pressure negatively associated with creative output, but creativity flagged for up to two days after deadlines, as people seemed to suffer what the researchers termed a post-deadline 'pressure hangover'.

Why is time important for idea development? Amabile points to 30 years of psychological research. Time is needed to explore a range of potentially useful concepts in relation to a specific challenge, to learn things that may prove useful, and to let the brain link concepts in unusual ways. Without the available time, one or more of these elements may be missing.

Leadership, Climate and Goodwill

The climate metaphor resonates quickly and powerfully with most people's experience of work. Since we spend so much of our time at work, and invest significant meaning in our work, and since knowledge–work presumes the willingness of the knowledge worker — so the perceived health of our workplace environment is key to developing our potential as humans.

Many things affect the health of team and organisational climates, including, but not limited to, the competitiveness of the marketplace, organisational policies, resource availability and task requirements. However, when one looks within an organisation, across different units, and holds constant the broader factors, so there emerge variations in the health of climates across teams, departments and divisions. And research suggests that the local leadership has the strongest effect on team climate creation.

Ekvall found that how leaders influence work colleagues, in formal or informal interactions, accounted for between 30% and 60% of the variance in climate for creativity.[10] Broader climate research concluded that between 53% and 72% of employees' perceptions of climate could be traced back to the leader.[11]

Leadership affects our perceptions of climate both directly and indirectly. Leaders directly affect employees' perception of climate through their impact on social and psychological processes such as problem solving, decision-making, communication, coordination, learning, commitment and motivation.[12] More indirectly, they affect climate through their attention to and use of a range of factors, including, but not limited to, organisational resources, systems, task design, mission and strategy.[3]

A poor climate can quite easily undermine existing capabilities. When organisations spend time and money on training people to produce creative ideas, and align these efforts to organisational priorities, but don't have supportive local climates — results often fall flat. For example, if people believe that the team leader will be critical of ideas, or can't see the connection to organisational needs, or is failing to tackle conflicts between team members — all of these are likely to affect climate for the worse, and to result in people withholding their best efforts.

Poor team climates are not uncommon. A Hay Group survey of more than 86,000 leaders worldwide found demotivating work climates present in more than 50% of teams across most of the world. North America was the best-performing region, with only 49% of leaders creating demotivating climates, 14% neutral, 15% energising and 22% high-performing.[13]

So how much does climate matter? The answer seems to be: quite a lot. Goleman argues that variations in organisational climate account for nearly a third of the impact on subsequent performance.[14] Clearly, wider economic conditions and the strategic competitive dynamics of the marketplace also matter enormously. But, this intra-organisational factor, with leadership at the core, is too large to ignore. As Stringer pointed out, in summarising decades of research on climate and organisational outcomes:

> What the boss of a work group does is the most important determinant of climate. The boss' behaviour drives climate, which arouses motivation. And aroused motivation is a major driver of bottom-line performance.[15] (p. 99)

The intervening aspect between climate and performance is our discretionary effort — the energy we choose to give, or withhold, to our work, over and above the minimum needed. And, crucially, climate health is at the heart of discretionary effort. In a positive, supportive, climate, we are prepared to give more. When the climate is more limiting, even punishing, people withdraw their extra energies, and act to survive, doing the minimum necessary. And in knowledge-based work, where creative outcomes are often expected, our goodwill is an increasingly important and intangible asset.

Climate and the Situational Outlook Questionnaire

If climate is so important, then how do we describe and define it? One of the main attempts to conceptualise the climate model for creativity, came from Goran Ekvall, a Swedish industrial psychologist.[16,17] Ekvall's foundational work was further developed, and nine key dimensions were identified. Isaksen describes how these dimensions were developed and applied at the individual, team and organisational levels.[3]

The dimensions have also been tested and found to distinguish between best- and worst-case work environments[18]; to predict higher perceived levels of support for organizational creativity and innovation[19]; and to discriminate between climates that are more stress free and have higher levels of job satisfaction.[3]

Let's look at these nine dimensions in more detail.

Challenge and involvement: The degree to which people are involved in daily operations and long-term goals. When this is high, people feel connected to the important goals of the organisation. Simply, their work matters. When it is low, people may feel apathetic about their work, or cynical about the future of the organisation.

Leaders may improve *challenge and involvement* by getting people involved in interpreting strategic organisational goals and connecting these to their daily roles. For example, one healthcare leader introduced regular story-telling sessions, where individual team members described how they'd taken action to make experiences better for their patients. These were discussed, learnt from, and the sessions became a way of integrating the team and reminding them of their purpose.

Freedom: The independence in behaviour exerted by the people in the organizations. This relates to the extent to which people have discretion over their work. When freedom is high, team members value that they are encouraged to gather information, set priorities and generate ideas for their own work plans. When this is low, people may spend too much time seeking permission for action. They may have given up and show very little initiative.

In practice, a common way for leaders to improve *freedom* in their team, is through themselves developing better coaching skills. Coaching requires leaders to think hard about engaging their people. One of the strategies for this is through encouraging team members to think through their own problem-solving strategies, with support, but not solutions, from the team leader.

Trust and openness: The emotional safety in relationships. This is one of the so-called 'soft' dimensions, but which has a hard impact. In teams where this is high, people know each other well enough, such that they understand each other's explicit and implicit needs. Where this is low, team members may not share ideas, for fear of them being 'stolen' by others, or others using ideas to further their own personal agendas.

A purchasing department was struggling, being led by a highly directive leader. His anxieties fuelled his unrelenting drive on high standards and zero errors. What he called perfectionism was perceived by others as unjust criticism. Without intending to do so, he had undermined trust, and people had withdrawn their best efforts. He was replaced by a new leader, and given a new role. The new leader brought people together to work on key departmental priorities. He increased interactions between people, and trust grew as people first learned to value each other's competence, and then the different skills they possessed.

Idea Time: The amount of time people can (and do) use for considering new ideas. In the last 5 years, lack of time for idea development has become the most commonly quoted obstacle to creativity and innovation. When this is low, teams are purely work focused, and unable to consider their own professional development. Energy and attention for new projects are curtailed, and people appear to have 'tunnel-vision'. When this dimension is high, there is more of a virtuous spiral between personal and team development, attending to new opportunities and turning ideas into action.

One healthcare team improved their score here by simply allocating time in weekly meetings to talk about priority work that required innovative ideas. The enjoyment from this session spread to other areas of work, and increased the demand for this way of working.

Humour and Spontaneity: The spontaneity and ease displayed within the workplace. Teams where this is low tend to focus on the transactional aspects of work. There is little rapport, and exchanges are more inhibited. Where this is high, people feel more relaxed, smile and laugh more.

Where teams improve on this dimension, they have sometimes reduced the repetitive, even duplicated aspects of their work, and build in more interactions between their people. When people feel safer with each other, and more at ease, they may start sharing their half-formed ideas, and things 'start to happen'. This type of restorative leadership takes proactivity and optimism, and it creates a contagious mood in the team.

Conflict: The presence of personal and emotional tensions in the organisation. This refers to tensions between people, often expressed as animosity, sometimes in corridor conversations. It is the only climate dimension where a higher score is undesirable. When it is high, it diverts energy away from the work. It is uncomfortable for other people to be in their presence of those in conflict. People may spend their energies anticipating the inevitable spat. When conflict is healthier, there is more focus on the work itself, rather than the dysfunctional relationships.

Smart leaders emphasise common, collaborative goals and the value of differences. And they see these as a resource, in support of a larger goal.

Idea Support: The ways in which new ideas are treated. Having time for idea development is one thing, but how those ideas are treated by others is another. When this is high, people are unafraid of sharing their undeveloped, initial thinking on ideas. They know that others will build on it and make it better. Where it is low, ideas may remain in people's heads, undeveloped and, usually, not implemented. Where ideas are shared, they may be shot down, leading to less sharing next time!

Training can help here. Few of us have learnt the skills of strengthening ideas, especially those which contain genuine novelty. Learning to point out the interesting and positive, before discussing the flaws, seems to encourage people to share more ideas. Also, because ideas often take time to develop, teams benefit from their leaders providing ways of protecting ideas from premature evaluation by more senior people. This helps breed safety and confidence to explore for genuinely novel solutions.

Debate: The occurrence of encounters and disagreements between viewpoints and ideas. Debate is about the sharing of diverse perspectives. It is different to conflict, because the focus here is on bringing together a diversity of perspectives to inform better debate. Where this is healthy, people get enjoyment from contributing to a better solution, with appreciative listening. Where debate is low, people may have learnt that their voice is unimportant. There may be plenty of complaining about work matters, but few productive conversations.

A simple and effective, though underappreciated, approach for leaders is to listen to others in order to understand. This can help to turn the climate around debate, so people learn that their views are important and sought. One Indian leader, of a global healthcare organisation, described how he tried to change the climate in his team. Previously, he was expected to have all the answers, and, plainly, this was unsustainable. It took three meetings for the expectations to start to change, and the debate to be more shared.

Risk taking: The tolerance of uncertainty and ambiguity exposed in the workplace. Risk taking refers to our capacity to acknowledge the uncertainties and ambiguities that are part of change, and act anyway. Ekvall thought that a high degree of risk taking was the dimension most predictive of radical innovation.

When this is low, teams may have experienced ideas not being turned into action in the past. As a consequence, few interesting ideas are proposed now. Where risk taking is high, there are often 'stretch' challenges and an importance placed on learning, both from mistakes and successes.

In practice, leaders often consider where their teams can experiment while acting to mitigate risks and undesirable consequences. They think thoughts like: not all mistakes affect desired outcomes in substantial ways; we can pilot approaches and learn without damaging our reputation and stakeholders' confidence; we can find room for action, where any errors can happen within acceptable boundaries.

In practice, when teams have developed the capacity for appropriate risk-taking, people often accept that some things will work whilst others will not, and they keep trying new approaches. They loosen up on the process, while being very focused on the goals. For them, simply, learning is work.

The SOQ Climate Tool

This climate framework has been operationalised through the development of an online diagnostic called the Situational Outlook Questionnaire (SOQ).[20] The questionnaire

- has developed benchmarks to distinguish between climates of stagnated and innovative organisations, and for most and least creative teams;
- combines 52 quantitative and 3 qualitative questions. The quantitative items are themed around the above nine dimensions, while the three qualitative are more open ended and ask for members' perceptions on what helps and hinders creativity, as well as what action they'd take to improve it in their team.

We have used the SOQ on many work programmes where creativity and innovation were needed by leaders and teams. The following cases and review are illustrative of the issues involved when leaders deliberately set out to improve work climate.

Case 1: Solverboard — The Open Innovation People

Context

Charlie Widdows is a co-founder of Solverboard, which is an open innovation business, based in Bristol, United Kingdom. The business started in 2015, focusing on inviting challenge owners to publicise their challenges on the Solverboard platform, and access people with challenge-solving ideas. These challenges might be placed within an organisation, across supply chains, or even 'open' to anyone wishing to send a potential solution.

Charlie describes working with Phil Atherton, who is the Founder for the organisation. Between them, Charlie and Phil are the senior organisational leaders of Solverboard.

We worked with Charlie, Phil and the Solverboard team, in November 2016, running a two-day innovation workshop. As preparation for the workshop, the team members completed the SOQ climate assessment, and

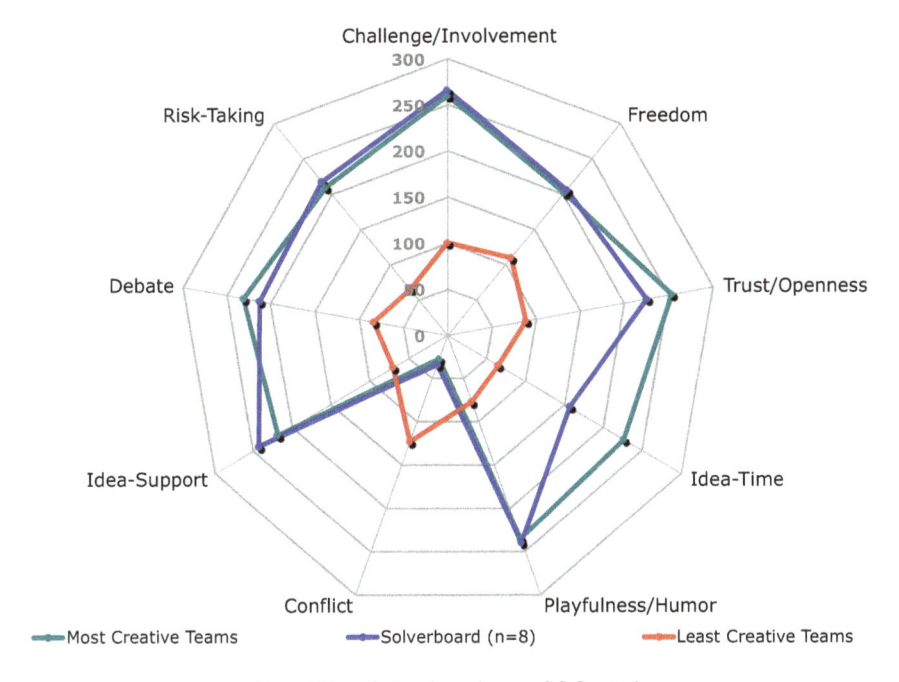

Figure 5.2: Solverboard team SOQ results

their results are shown below. The blue line shows the Solverboard overall profile, compared to the green benchmarks for most creative teams, and the red benchmark for least creative teams. The stand-out area for improvement is Idea-Time, while most other results are good.

Much of the interview concentrates on what Charlie and Phil decided, following the workshop, and how they've worked with the team to improve climate and performance in the subsequent months. The results are showed in Figure 5.2.

Rob: In November 2016, we worked with you, and looked at the SOQ results for your team. The overall results were very good, but not for Idea-Time.

Charlie: I think this is the conundrum of a business trying to run before it can walk. We have so much to do, but we were finding ourselves spending our lives chasing our tails and fighting fires. (I think here of the Apple Store. They could squeeze more people in there, but they choose not to — they want people to have space and time to weigh up how they could use these products. They want people to have a brand experience that makes them feel good.) Our problem pre-workshop, was that we weren't giving ourselves time to think.

Rob: Were the results a surprise?

Charlie: No, they weren't, but they were something we hadn't really thought about. We'd been fiercely protective of our culture, but we were uncomfortable with long silences — 'does this mean I don't look busy?...' So, we kept ourselves very busy.

One of the things that helped me think differently about this was working with an advertising agency. The people there are very protective of thinking time. And what we're trying to get to with Solverboard is just that: you go into a branded space, and you recognise people, and this becomes a 'place to go'. We'd been guilty of not creating that place to go for ourselves.

Rob: So, since the workshop, what have you done to change what you wanted around time for developing ideas?

Charlie: First, we realised that, like with any start-up, there's a hell of a lot to do. Solverboard is built on some principles for its effective use: leadership involvement and leaders leading. Phil and I decided, at Xmas 2016, to give ourselves more time to think and to weigh up our options.

We also realised that our people are always thinking about the work anyway. So, it doesn't matter about having to work in front of each other. Phil and I particularly, we're always thinking about how to make Solverboard better. There were three key learnings: you're always 'on' — so it doesn't matter if you're not always present. Which was very liberating and took the pressure off, massively. Second, realising that we can't do everything, and things won't fall over and break. Third, we considered how to apply these points to the team and the workspace.

Rob: And how did you do these?

Charlie: We agreed that Phil would take some time off in the summer. And we'd both try not to work until midnight, and weekends, etc. We said to each other that we'd aim for a better balance. And we told the team this. We said that: in order to do your best work, find a balance.

But before this, we looked at roles and responsibilities. Previously, we had a lot of the team say: 'I'll pick that up...' which was great at the time, but it meant that lines of accountability got blurred, and that looking at people's performance was harder, because the limits of their work were unclear. So, we implemented more focus and structure through clearer roles and responsibilities. Which meant we could appraise people on the quality of the work they were doing. Which meant they could self-govern.

It also meant that we could employ people better than us, in their area of quality. Plus it created a relaxed, friendly, working environment where they want to come to work. This gives people the freedom to achieve their work, in their own way.

Rob: Do you genuinely feel OK about employing people better than you?

Charlie: Yes, I'd much rather be the Chris Froome (solidly good at many things) than the Mark Cavendish (specialised sprinter). Phil and I had put in a lot of work in the first two years — we put in solid foundations for this. We also realised we couldn't do it on our own, so we asked: Where do we need strengthening? And we thought: in our content, sales, product and technical development and so on. You can't be all things. What we realised is, we're good at managing clusters of those people and setting the rules for how we work, to get the best from those people.

So, for example, Aaron is an unbelievably good salesman, but he's also a great helper. That may be in helping people in the team, and the client. He knows that an attribute of client development is being genuinely helpful, the net result of which is that the client stays longer, and revenue goes up. That means that he, too, is 'always on' and that doesn't change if he's working from home, in the office or wherever. He's always working hard.

It's funny: you have to be quite self-confident to say you're working with people better than you. I think I'm good at managing upwards, sideways and clients. Therefore, that gives me the right to say I want someone better than me at sales. But I'll sit here and make sure they integrate well.

Rob: So, 9 months later, after the climate measurement, what difference do you think it's made so far?

Charlie: First, it's made a difference to Solverboard's success. We're increasing users and revenue month by month. All parts of the engine are working well. Also, the office environment has improved. We work with other business in our building, and they notice our climate and morale. We have a fortnightly meeting to share what we're doing. People look forward to the Solverboard part of that. We're a two year-old company, and working with some fantastic clients. All of these things have happened because the environment reflects our business, and there's a gentle hum of activity to say: all these constituent parts are working in harmony.

Rob: It sounds more coherent and less frantic?

Charlie: We're fighting less fires and being less frantic — which doesn't look good to anyone. We're more ordered and have created more space for ideas to thrive. If there was one takeaway from the training it was: How do we change and implement that? And we have. It's fundamentally changed how we're prepared to work. It's allowed us to admit that business doesn't equal productivity.

Case Review

In this case, the team's climate results were generally very good, with the glaring exception of idea time. Charlie describes a fundamental shift of mindset in the team, initiated at senior leadership level. The frantic nature of start-ups, and the initial goodwill of people can lead to a generalised culture of saying 'yes' and acting well beyond one's role. Solverboard had reached the point where people were feeling slightly overstretched.

This state of affairs can creep up over time. Charlie describes not being surprised by the low score on idea time, but that he and others had not thought about it consciously and with a deliberate, serious intent to change it. The timing of the training was well chosen in this regard. He and Phil set out to implement changes to the business in 2017.

They realised that, as leaders, they had to model the climate that they wanted for others. And they realised that their earlier practices of working long hours were creating a 'ripple' effect on others. That was not helpful for incubating and developing ideas.

They brought more focus and boundaries to people's roles, as well as more freedom in how people could choose to do their work. This is an interesting example of how constraints can bring more choice. The norms of work changed in that people were encouraged to think about their own productivity, and how to achieve this — to take responsibility for their own performance.

Having clarified roles, Charlie also describes a dynamic of employing talented people, who are excellent — better than him — in their own domains. In order to be the most productive, the challenge became how to provide the work environment most suitable to sustain everyone's goodwill, and deliver results?

And the results are starting to change. Others are noticing the climate and morale of the team; employee productivity seems higher, client interest is expanding, and revenue is increasing.

Case 2: The Healthcare Unit

Background and context

This case looks at two leaders in a healthcare organisation, based in a regional centre in the United Kingdom. Jane had recently become leader of the Podiatry leadership team, and Simon was a member of that team. Simon reported to Jane, and he also led a team which was implementing a change in service approach to diabetes.

The case focuses on two periods: April 2013–January 2014, which is when Jane attended a leadership programme, and November 2014–May 2015, which is when Simon attended a separate healthcare leadership programme.

Both people were in leadership roles, and in positions to apply their learning. And both leadership programmes contained a strong element of learning about innovation. We also measured their respective team climates, using the SOQ, at the start and end of these leadership programmes.

In August 2017, I interviewed both leaders together for this case. An unusual aspect of this case is that it shows how learning about climate was carried across two different teams over a nearly-two-year time period (see Table 5.1).

Table 5.1: Podiatry leadership team initial climate results

Dimensions	Most creative team experience ($n = 170$)	Least creative team experience ($n = 170$)	First-time averages (April 2013)
Challenge	260	100	210
Freedom	202	110	169
Trust and openness	253	88	193

(Continued)

Table 5.1: (Continued)

Dimensions	Most creative team experience ($n = 170$)	Least creative team experience ($n = 170$)	First-time averages (April 2013)
Idea time	227	65	108
Playfulness	235	77	200
Conflict	27	123	44
Idea support	218	70	203
Debate	231	83	192
Risk taking	210	65	150

(Source for most and creative team data sources, Ref. [20])

Phase 1: The podiatry leadership team

On becoming the new leader of the overall unit, Jane had introduced a role and structure review. This led to some people taking redefined roles, with some reductions in salary. There had also been one redundancy and morale had dropped.

Table 5.1 shows the April 2013 quantitative results. The SOQ qualitative feedback from this report showed that the main factors hindering creativity were lack of time and people resources, with accompanying high clinical caseloads. At the same time, team members appreciated the support, both from their peers and from the team leader, Jane. When asked what they most desired to increase creativity in the team, the most common response was: protected time for developing and implementing ideas.

Rob: Having received the initial SOQ results for the podiatry leadership team, at start of programme, what hit home to you?

Jane: I was interested to see that there were reasonably positive results. But also, Challenge and Involvement, Freedom, Idea time, Playfulness and Humour were low. So, I created myself a SOQ roadmap: a programme of changes for the team that I thought would influence climate.

Rob: So, that was quite a deliberate programme?

Jane: Yes, I knew the leadership evidence was there, about climate and innovation, but it's not the same as clinical evidence. I had a lot of confidence in the team. A lot invested in it. I was new to the role. I'd restructured them all, and a lot of what I was doing was unknown to me. I was feeling my way, and had to do something. But, also, I saw lots of opportunities ahead of us.

Rob: It sounds like you had a deliberate focus on team climate improvement. How did you apply what you were learning?

Jane: First, we worked on challenge and involvement. I took the strategic vision of the organisation, and made it accessible to the team. We started to create themes and objectives for our services that aligned to the strategic needs of the organisation.

We used creative problem-solving tools to generate over 300 ideas. From this, the team reduced these to 10 team objectives, connected with our wider organisational strategy and vision. The team hadn't worked in this way before, and the process had the unexpected benefit of bringing more openness to the team.

Rob: So, people learnt more about how their work fitted with wider organisational goals. What else did you do?

Jane: We did a lot of problem solving and idea-generation sessions. I built time into the service to do that. I eliminated other work and put these in. I spent quite a lot of time coaching and encouraging you (talking to Simon) to take the same approach with other people. I wanted to give the team leaders the autonomy to solve their own problems and understand the environment and tools to negotiate with their teams. We'd use creative problem-solving tools in our meetings, and I encouraged my team members to share this work with their own teams. I think this shared the importance of the work with the wider organisation, and also spread the importance of working creatively.

And then we embedded the changes. We followed through with ideas and supported people to implement changes. Of the 10 top priorities, 7 have been completed. We drove them through quickly, to create some pace.

Simon: It also created a sense that 'we're doing something' with the rest of the team.

Jane: I was realising that people may have felt stifled in the past by a more hierarchical leadership structure. I wanted to raise people's interest in what we were doing. I sent out a 360-feedback request, every 6 months. I encouraged people to challenge us. We created a very public meeting with more than 70 of our people from our different teams. At the end of those sessions, the leadership team would stand and we'd ask: 'what questions have you got, and what do you want to know from us?'

Rob: And did they ask?

Simon: Yes, they did. It was nerve wracking for us. Not knowing what would come out. But, once you've done one, it was fine.

Jane: Regardless of how tough was the issue, or how uncomfortable the response might be I took time to provide the responses required. If I did not know the answers to the questions I admitted it and suggested ways in which we might solve the problem and answer the question together.

Simon (talking to Jane): We needed to develop our trust in you. We'd heard your reputation because podiatry is a small world. But you, being open, and sharing all this strategic stuff — that helped build trust.

Rob (to Simon): What did it feel like to you, as a member of this leadership team?

Simon: It felt like, 'Ok, I'm going with this!' I think your enthusiasm helped (pointing to Jane).

Jane: The hardest thing was risk taking. The level of bureaucracy in a clinical organisation — it is difficult to overcome. So, we took risks in a measured way. We developed small wins with the team and this has been of critical importance in demonstrating a measured approach to risk taking.

Through this process we identified opportunities and created a £330,000 bid for funding to extend our diabetes services. It was a gamble, because we didn't have enough data to know how it would work out. I did a lot of managing upwards to reassure people that we could do this.

Rob: What did you notice in this time, Simon, about people's energy and whether they were prepared to give more?

Simon: We were a new team together, and I had to support my own team, who were reporting to me. I wanted to increase my team's skillset and make them feel more supported. You absorb whatever tools seem to be working. It was about building trust with everybody. We were doing exercises, interacting with each other and playing games, and we hadn't seen anything like that for a long time. You led us (speaking to Jane) and that was telling, given where we'd come from, with our previous leadership. We'd been stagnant for many years.

Rob: And, looking at the effect of learning, would you have done all of these things anyway, even if you hadn't come on the leadership programme?

Jane: I think it's about confidence. On the leadership programme, I was sitting there with more senior leaders, and you could see that the tools made an impact on these people. And, as time passed, I understood that my style of doing things had as much credence as theirs. And, in that environment, you could test the tools and try them out with a group of people — that was useful and gave me confidence to try them with my team in real settings.

Rob: And, in this period of time, what changes did you introduce?

Jane: We created a culture of skills and quality. We implemented a framework of clinical competencies for us to develop across podiatry; put in a clinical supervision process, to help us evaluate and develop our skills; created a coaching culture, designed to help and inspire our team members; we introduced a zero-tolerance approach to completing 1:1 appraisals — everyone had a 1:1 appraisal! We also introduced educational talks for practice nurses who were dealing with patients suffering from diabetes. We also won £330,000 of funding to extend our diabetes service provision. And we set ourselves a 4-week target for seeing all patients after their referral.

Phase 1 review

In a nine-month period, there were many improvements in the climate dimensions, as can be seen in Table 5.2.

The qualitative data from the SOQ also reflected the improvement in climate:

> I think the idea support in this team is great. (Our) team is excellent at working together in creating innovative solutions to solving problems. The level of trust in the team is very high. Creative problem-solving techniques are used early to predict future opportunities and solve existing issues.

Lack of time and high workload pressures are still a key issue. However, the shift of focus of concern seems to be beyond the team. Several team members point to the demands on the team that have been initiated from outside. This distinction between in-team and the wider organisation seems to have sharpened:

Table 5.2: Podiatry leadership team repeat climate results

Dimensions	Most creative team experience ($n = 170$)	Least creative team experience ($n = 170$)	First time averages (April 2013, $n = 6$)	Second time averages (Jan 2014, $n = 6$)
Challenge	260	100	210	264
Freedom	202	110	169	200
Trust and openness	253	88	193	233
Idea time	227	65	108	156
Playfulness	235	77	200	256
Conflict	27	123	44	25
Idea support	218	70	203	260
Debate	231	83	192	197
Risk taking	210	65	150	200

(Our) Creativity (is) hampered by lack of incentive, this is external to the team but resonates in the organisation as a whole. The creative team dynamic is good and quite healthy — the (wider) organisation entrepreneurship not very good.

It is easy to see, from the above interview, that Jane had identified that a change of leadership approach was required. Morale was suffering, partly through the recent restructuring, and high workload levels, and, perhaps, as a legacy of the previous leadership style.

She realised that she needed the willing buy-in of her staff. She set out to engage her leadership team, through coaching, joint working, creative thinking sessions and encouraging them to cascade such thinking and action with their own teams. This took considerable effort and time, and the pay-off seems to have been high, as judged by the changes introduced and the high climate scores.

Phase 2: The Diabetic Bid Implementation Team

Rob: What about your story, Simon, because you did the later leadership programme?

Simon: We knew we'd be getting the £330,000 coming in from our successful funding bid. We knew we'd have to change how we worked on diabetes services, so the timing was good. It was a huge change.

The work that Jane had put into us with the initial team — many of those were in the diabetic implementation team (see Table 5.3). My emphasis was in maintaining that good climate as much as possible. And making us productive, generating solutions and planning.

Jane: Is there an issue of the grind of implementation versus creating something new? It's slower burn...

Simon: It is, but it's still exciting. I did a lot of coaching through 1:1s with my team. Jane is good at coaching me to coach them, and I'm living it day to day.

Rob: As is often the case, time sounds like a main challenge. How did you keep things 'open' enough for what you needed?

Simon. I was thinking: 'we don't have the luxury of time, so how can we manage it effectively?' We made sure we were protected from the hustle and bustle of everyday work. We'd use clinical rooms so people didn't know where we were. We engaged the team constantly, and used ideas from them, to get their buy in, from the ground up.

Jane: Overall, with this team, we made a massive impact on patients. We reduced the time from doctor's referral to clinical appointment for diagnosis. But, we also created a problem for ourselves, by identifying an unmet need, which wasn't covered by the funding. In our geography, there's a low diagnosis rate for type 2 diabetes, and a high limb amputation rate. We were not diagnosing patients early enough, which means that condition-complications happen. By the time you're diagnosed, your trajectory can be difficult, and the route to lower limb amputation is quite quick. We've pushed that down by quite a lot, I think.

Rob. You were victims of your success by spotting an undealt-with need. This raised the demand for your services, but you didn't have the capacity to deal with it, under the existing funding arrangements.

Jane: The funding we were awarded, was less than was needed, to deal with the size of the problem. The original bids were nearly three times what was eventually awarded. Though we introduced an improvement, it meant that demand increased to the point where we couldn't see people as quickly as we wanted.

Rob: In your story, Simon, you inherited an engaged team for an important piece of work, and implemented a plan. By the end of the leadership course, you'd kept the climate healthy. How much of a difference do you think that made to the quality of your work?

Simon: I think it's huge. We needed the buy-in from everyone in that team, to support all their staff. It's really important.

Rob: And, it can be hard to attribute impact, but what impact do you think your way of working had had on patients?

Simon: They have more accessibility when they need it. We've done two focus groups with our diabetes cohorts and developed a diabetes risk line. It's a game-changer. They'll ring us and speak to a clinician, and get their problem sorted either over the phone or be signposted. The feedback from patients has been nothing but positive. Hearing stories from patients makes a big difference to us. And that was one of the ideas from the work as a result of the £330,000 funding.

Rob: What kind of scale are we talking about? The number of people who've benefitted?

Jane: Around 4,500 patients will be having more regular diabetic foot-check reviews. Also, I think that this project was a basis for more changes. As soon as the commissioners invested, they saw an improvement and realised they had to do more. The ripple effect of this project has had, I think, a huge impact on what they (the commissioners) are considering important.

Rob: Are you seeing any measurable, clinical changes in outcomes for your patients?

Simon: At the moment the amputation data is backdated. We think the next data will show that it has decreased. (So, it's too early to know for sure.)

Table 5.3: Diabetic implementation team, initial and repeat climate results

Dimensions	Most creative team experience ($n = 170$)	Least creative team experience ($n = 170$)	First-time averages (November 2014)	Second-time averages (May 2015)
Challenge	260	100	257	267
Freedom	202	110	200	186

(Continued)

Table 5.3: (Continued)

Dimensions	Most creative team experience (n = 170)	Least creative team experience (n = 170)	First-time averages (November 2014)	Second-time averages (May 2015)
Trust and openness	253	88	227	217
Idea time	227	65	136	150
Playfulness	235	77	233	250
Conflict	27	123	61	39
Idea support	218	70	220	243
Debate	231	83	208	206
Risk taking	210	65	227	203

Phase 2 review

Simon has clearly applied learning from the earlier experience with Jane. He understands the process and importance of building ideas from the 'ground up'. And of using a coaching approach to help engage people, individually, on a day by day basis. The idea for the diabetes risk line has come from talking directly with patients, and seems to be having a positive effect, even if this feedback is anecdotal only, while impact data is being collected.

Simon has maintained an already good climate, protecting time for idea development, in a context where pressures often come top-down.

Interestingly, this case throws up an example of how teams may create challenges for themselves. Because of their far-sightedness, the team had identified that type 2 diabetes sufferers were not being dealt with early enough, and this delayed diagnosis might be affecting later treatment options. However, having identified the root of this particular problem, the team did not have the internal resources to deal with the consequences. Complex problems sometimes need complex collaboration to solve them.

Chapter Review — Key Learning on Creating a Healthy Climate

There are several things that leaders find helpful when they measure and set out to improve team climate. First, having team feedback against relevant benchmarks gives leaders and teams a meaningful focus on priorities. Second, it channels their energies within their field of influence. Third, given the depth of research on the relationships between climate and team performance, it gives them confidence that working to improve climate will bring improvement in team innovation outcomes in their own context.

In practice, we have worked with leaders who have improved their team's work climate for innovation within 9–12 months, and found that climate is a 'lead' indicator of innovation performance. Manage the team climate and the results will follow.

But for a small minority of teams, climate even worsened through a nine-month period. Why was this? When we spoke to the team leaders, the most common issue was that they lacked sufficiently strong relationships with more senior people, outside their teams. For some, this was their immediate line manager. For others, it was a key senior stakeholder. Because of this, they couldn't leverage the influence they needed to give their teams protected exploration time and couldn't galvanise each other around agreed and meaningful innovation goals. Clearly, the team unit is important as a source where ideas are developed. But implementation often takes place in the social and political context of the wider organisation, and without the required support, changes will not be sustainable.

Note how Jane, in the second case described above, put time and effort into reassuring more senior leadership that her team could handle the increased scale of their work. She was successful in these influence efforts.

What effective leaders know about climate is that

1. they are affecting it anyway, so they'd better make their impact positive;
2. they can help it improve, and fairly quickly;

3. most importantly, climate makes the difference to people wanting to give their best, over time. Without a positive climate, initiatives come and go. And with knowledge workers, their willingness is all-important.

Leaders must be self-aware, to understand how they're affecting the work climate for others. And flexible through their influence to affect it the way they want. Interdependent-minded leaders create positive climates in a number of ways.

First, they accept that they need the skills and talents of the people in their team, to initiate and sustain change over time. Their thoughts of mutuality in relationships compel them to think of creating a positive climate that will help apply the skills of the whole team. Experience of working with climate as a concept also suggests that views of climate tend to become more positive, further up the organisational hierarchy. Knowing this, effective leaders will genuinely want to know how others perceive the climate at lower levels in the organisation.

Second, they accept the nature of change in its complexity. Change often arouses mixed, and sometimes opposing, emotions in people: excitement, apprehension regarding the unknown, optimism and hope for the future, fear of losing out and so on. Mature leaders accept the complexities of this differentiated state and acknowledge it. Acknowledging this publicly seems to lower the pressure valve on change, and bring space for creative thinking and action.

Third, in practice, this leads to bounded experimentation taking place. Team members want to introduce changes, not for the thrill of change, but to serve a meaningful work purpose. And they take time to work out the tactics of doing so, while minimising any potential negative consequences.

References

1. Koestler, A. (1940). *Darkness at Noon*. London: Penguin Books.
2. Alon, A. *et al*. (2012). Accenture. Available at: https://www.accenture.com/us-en/insight-outlook-art-of-managing-innovation-risk.aspx (Accessed on 23/11/2017).

3. Isaksen, S. G. (2017). Leadership's Role in Creative Climate Creation. In: *Handbook of Research on Leadership and Creativity* by Mumford, M. and Hemlin, S. (Eds.), pp. 131–158. Cheltenham: Edward Elgar.
4. Puccio, G. J., Murdock, M. C., and Mance, M. (2007). *Creative Leadership: Skills that Drive Change.* Thousand Oaks, CA: Sage.
5. Byrne, C. L., Mumford, M. D., Barrett, J. D., and Vessey, W. B. (2009). "Examining the Leaders of Creative Efforts: What Do They Do, and What Do They Think About?" *Creativity and Innovation Management* 18(4): 256–268.
6. Oldham, G. R. and Cummings, A. (1996). "Employee Creativity: Personal and Contextual Factors at Work." *Academy of Management Journal* 39: 607–634.
7. Claxton, G. (1998). *Hare Brain, Tortoise Mind: Why Intelligence Increases When You Think Less.* London: Fourth Estate.
8. Isen, A., Daubman, K. and Nowicki, G. (1987). "Positive Affect Facilitates Creative Problem Solving." *Journal of Personality and Social Psychology* 52(6): 1122–1131.
9. Amabile, T. M. (2002). "Creativity Under the Gun." *Harvard Business Review* August: 52–61.
10. Ekvall, G. (1999). Creative Climate. In: *Encyclopedia of Creativity*, Vol. 1, Runco, M. A. and Pritzker S. R. (Eds.), pp. 403–412. San Diego, CA: Academic Press.
11. Kelner, S. P. *et al.* (1996). Managerial Style as a Predictor of Organizational Climate. Boston: McBer and Co.
12. Isaksen, S. *et al.* (2001). "Perceptions of the Best and Worst Climates for Creativity: Preliminary Validation Evidence for the Situational Outlook Questionnaire." *Creativity Research Journal* 13 (2): 171–184.
13. Hay Group. Available at: http://atrium.haygroup.com/us/our-products/misc.aspx?ID=3698 (Accessed on 12/12/2017).
14. Goleman, D. (2000). "Leadership That Gets Results." *Harvard Business Review*, March–April: 78–90.
15. Stringer, R. (2002). *Leadership and Organizational Climate.* New Jersey: Prentice Hall.
16. Ekvall, G. (1983). *Climate, Structure and Innovativeness in Organizations: A Theoretical Framework and an Experiment.* Stockholm: Faradet.
17. Ekvall, G. (1987). The Climate Metaphor in Organization Theory. In: *Advances in Organizational Psychology* by Bass, B. M. and Drenth, P. J. (Eds.), pp. 177–190. Newbury Park, CA: Sage.

18. Isaksen, S. *et al.* (2001). "Perceptions of the Best and Worst Climates for Creativity: Preliminary Validation Evidence for the Situational Outlook Questionnaire." *Creativity Research Journal* 13(2): 171–184.
19. Rasulzada, F. and Dackert, I. (2009). "Organizational Creativity and Innovation in Relation to Psychological Well-being and Organizational Factors." *Creativity Research Journal* 21: 191–198.
20. Isaksen, S. G. and Lauer, K. CPSB. Available at: http://www.cpsb.com/research/articles/climate-for-innovation/Team-Climate-CIM.html (Accessed on 23/09/2017).

Chapter 6

Making Use of Different Perspectives

...I'm worried that I'm losing whatever creativity I've got.

(2010, early 20-something male, in a global professional services firm)

We were talking about his longer-term career, in the context of a two-day client-skills programme. He explained that, outside of his very busy work life, he liked to write songs and do photography. He seemed to value his artistic interests. More than that, he identified with them — he saw these pursuits as part of how he defined himself. But time for these interests was lacking while he was becoming professionally qualified. The strictures of his work didn't allow him to express himself creatively, and he was not at ease with himself. I tried to reassure him. I said that the piece of the jigsaw missing, right now, was opportunity. But, not to worry, his ways of thinking would remain and he would be able to reignite his passion for these interests in due course.

It takes effort and joint meaning making to connect innovation strategies to everyday work. Creative problem-solving skills can be learnt and applied in weeks and months, though continual development needs to be sustained. And team climate can be measurably improved in months. With all those innovation capabilities in place, ideas also need a range of perspectives, to access and generate different options through the creative problem-solving process (see Figure 6.1). This chapter looks at the application of Dr. Michael Kirton's adaption-innovation (A-I) theory of thinking-style differences.

Figure 6.1: ABCD model — Leverage the diversity of your people

Research Overview: The Role of Adaption-innovation Theory in Creative Problem Solving

Michael Kirton developed A-I theory, with its origin in the 1960s,[1] publishing the first book in 1976,[2] and another in 2003.[3] It has been the subject of considerable research by the academic community over four decades, with over 300 articles being written about it.[4]

A-I is fundamentally a theory of thinking style, applied to problem solving. Kirton distinguished between opportunity, motive, level and style. *Opportunity* is provided by the environment in which we work and live. The challenge here is one of perception, as many opportunities (or threats) are likely to co-exist, but, without us perceiving them, there is no subsequent problem solving.

Motive provides the process by which we concentrate, channel and direct our energies towards the goal. It relates to our intensity and persistence in pursuing that goal. Motive also helps explain why we choose some opportunities rather than others. Some opportunities appeal to us, intellectually and emotionally, more than others.

Having chosen the problem to address, Kirton distinguishes between level and style. *Level* describes the capacity we bring, and can include technical, leadership and interpersonal skills as well as experience. It can also include specific skills in working through the creative problem-solving process.

Style refers to the manner in which we solve problems. Kirton defines style as the 'strategic, stable characteristic — the preferred way in which people respond to and seek to bring about change'. In other words, how we prefer to work through the process of solving problems.[3]

One of Kirton's main contributions was to show that level and style are unrelated. Having more or less capacity says nothing about the characteristic style in which we solve problems.

A-I theory focuses on style: the differences in how people use cognitive structure to solve problems. The core of the difference in styles revolves around the degree of structure people prefer to use. People with a more adaptive preference prefer to use more structure through the problem-solving process; whereas people with a more innovative preference prefer to use less structure. And, as we will see, these differences can have important consequences for effectiveness and collaboration in problem solving.

For example, the more adaptive prefer to work within the bounds of the prevailing structure, and to appreciate its proven, enabling potential. They are less sensitive to the current structure's limiting aspects. They are also more likely to wish to establish a tighter structure, (before the more innovative), because they appreciate the potential of structure for extracting value to solve the problems at hand. The more adaptive are also more likely to gain a consensus between people, as they proceed. Consensus is another type of structure — a social one.

Their value is clear: they are able to produce solutions that can be implemented within the prevailing approach, and to do so quickly and reliably. They are particularly strong at refining the standards and procedures of existing structures to make them more efficient. All people introduce change, and the more adaptive will bend and, if persuaded, break the structure, usually as an outcome of the problem-solving process. One of the potential 'blind-spots' for the more adaptive is that they may persevere with an existing structure for too long — after its value has receded.

The more innovative find the existing structure more limiting (and sooner than the more adaptive). They are more likely to detach a problem from its customary frame of reference, and redefine the nature of the problem. They may perceive the existing structure as being part of the problem, or even to be the cause of the problem. They are much more likely to change the prevailing structure in order to solve the problem, rather than as an outcome of having solved it. They are also more likely to be challenging. As their problem defining and solution generating may produce unexpected insights, these can discomfort their more adaptive colleagues. Their thoughts are challenging because they are often unexpected, and bring existing approaches into question. The more adaptive might take this challenge personally. Whether innovators deliver their challenge with sensitivity to the recipients is outside the scope of A-I theory, but undoubtedly has an impact on the resulting conversation.

Their value is in being to provide an insight that may more radically change the structure. Through not being so constrained by thinking within existing parameters, they are more likely to suggest solutions that bring in ideas from very different sources, and from beyond the boundaries where the current problem is located. The potential disadvantages of their approach include bringing solutions that may be more risky, harder to secure agreement, and a tendency to change the existing approach, even when it is still delivering value.

It's easy to see how differences in approach between the above styles can lead to disagreements on how to proceed. Kirton's point is that what is required depends on the nature of the problem. A more tightly defined problem, requiring an incremental solution, will need more of an adaptive approach. A more open-ended approach, with fewer prescriptions on how to proceed, will require a less structured, innovative approach.

The theory is operationalised in research studies through Kirton's development of a diagnostic questionnaire called the 'KAI', which stands for: Kirton's Adaption-innovation Inventory. This measures our preference point, along a continuum of possibilities, ranging from highly adaptive to highly innovative. Scores for large groups are distributed along a continuum from highly adaptive at one end, to highly innovative at the other. Typically, scores are spread in a normal distribution with more tending towards the centre, and increasingly fewer to the poles.

Given enough people in a sample size, the distribution of scores will reveal a normal distribution pattern. Scores range from theoretical maximum highs on adaption of 32 and on innovation of 160, with a population mean of 96.

It's also worth noting that Kirton is clear that people are neither adaptors nor innovators in his theory. We are simply more adaptive or innovative than someone else, which reflects the continuous range of the scores in a population. The point here is that the data is continuous. People don't fall into categories of adaptive or innovative. With one group, your profile may make you a strong innovator, while with another a moderate adaptor (see Figure 6.2).

It's easy to see that we are simply more or less adaptive and innovative than others. Take the following examples:

- Someone with a KAI preference of, say, 107 will be more innovative than around 75% of people and more adaptive than 25% of people.
- Another person with a KAI preference of 83 will be more adaptive than 75% of people and more innovative than 25%.

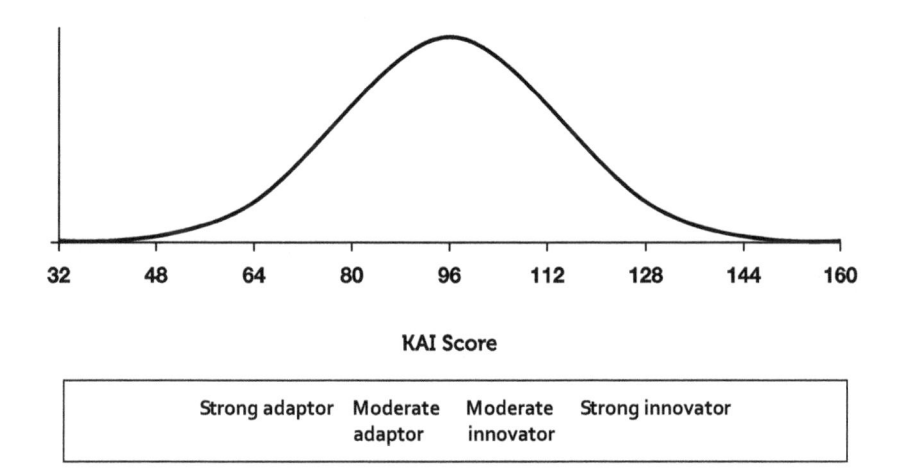

Figure 6.2: Results distribution for KAI profiles

Experience in working through feedback on this instrument with teams suggests that most people are not surprised at their scores. Around 80% of people are fairly accurate in anticipating their results. Some 20% are genuinely surprised, which often leads them to reflect on the current 'fit' between their style and both their work and the cultural expectations in their workplace.

Paradox of structure

Since structure is so fundamental to the theory, let's look at what Kirton describes as the paradox of structure. Each field tends to accumulate its own context-specific set of terms denoting structure. In the organisational world, concepts such as value processes, policies, procedures, role and organisational structures, cultural norms, with their explicit and implicit rules, can all be thought of as contributing to the structures people experience in work. In Kirton's theory, the paradox of structure is that every structure is both enabling and limiting at the same time. If people perceive a structure to be more enabling than limiting, then it has a better chance of surviving longer. And, as discussed above, the more innovative are more likely to point out the flaws in the existing structure; indeed, how the structure itself may contribute to, or even be, the problem. Whereas the more adaptive are more likely to see the value of existing structures for solving the problems at hand.

Cognitive gap and coping

A-I theory is explicit in saying that everyone is capable of being creative. Also, there is no generally better or worse style. What style is appropriate depends on the nature of the agreed problem, and effective collaboration with the people working on the problem.

The term cognitive gap can be thought of as a distance between the thinking that is required for effectiveness and what is available. Therefore, there may be two types of cognitive gap: between the style of the person, the nature of the problem and between the different styles of thinking of the people working on the problem.

A-I theory also argues, importantly, that our style preference does not change. It is an early set, stable characteristic. It is also clear that people learn coping behaviour: that is, to 'stretch' away from their preferred style, because the problem and/or group demands it. Kirton claims that such coping is fuelled by motive — a wish to meet the needs of the situation — and aided by coping strategies we have learnt over time. (We'll look more at these in the section below.) He also argues that coping takes significant effort and that increasing coping distance from one's preferred style is stressful, especially when it persists over time.

Experience shows that a 10-point difference between people will be noticed as differences in approach. A 20-point difference requires much more work, understanding and mutual respect for the difference to prove beneficial. Gaps beyond these require steeply increasing, not linear, efforts from both parties.

For effective problem solving, gaps in thinking styles between people are usually desirable because complex problems often require a range of thinking styles. The issue then becomes one of how to harness those differences for mutual benefit, rather than difference leading to interpersonal conflict and entrenched opposition.

Managing cognitive diversity

Kirton noted that differences were often accompanied with value judgements: if I'm successful and you're different, then you're inferior. In other words, differences can become personalised and positions easily entrenched. And while the rhetoric around the need for diverse teams is becoming louder, the experience of working in them can be different. Kurtzberg found that while diverse teams scored better on a measure of idea-fluency, working in these teams was often uncomfortable for team members, and team members didn't necessarily believe they were creative. What it *felt like* to be in the team had a greater impact on their assessment of their own creativity than did their actual creative output.[5]

This is consistent with Kirton's view — that it will be difficult to integrate too great a degree of difference, and that the greater the diversity, the greater the discomfort.[2]

Kirton described two types of problem: Problem A, where the person or group is focused on trying to solve the agreed problem. Problem B refers to people figuring out how to work with each other, in order to solve Problem A. As a broad rule, more time spent on Problem A is a 'good thing'. But teams also have to spend enough time on Problem B — understanding each other well enough, to build trust for exploration into novelty, and to understand the very differences they bring that can be useful.

As we've seen in earlier chapters, that complexity of challenges seems to be increasing. Where these problems bring a range of challenges over time — more adaptive and more innovative — then it is important to match this complexity with a diversity of thinking styles. The challenge is to make the best of this diversity. And while that may sound obvious, good practice in doing so is not common, and the spread of good practice is partial.

Story: Experimenting with the KAI

In an experimental exercise with Open University MBA alumni, we set up groups of strong adaptors, strong innovators and a diverse group. These were people who'd already encountered A-I theory through their programme, had received personal KAI feedback and reflected on the implications.

We gave them the task of pitching to a panel an idea for a new business, including some elaboration on how the business would make money. The panel's role was to choose their preferred idea using three criteria: idea novelty, the potential for the idea delivering profit and which team they trusted to deliver the idea to the marketplace. The panel itself comprised a diverse team, using KAI scores.

Typically, the most innovative team delivered their presentation with brio and flair. Their idea was, without fail, highly novel, while the detail on how they'd bring it to the marketplace was usually unconvincing. And, often, their delivery was accompanied by laughter, high volume and awareness of their lack of interest in detail. The adaptive group gave a solid, credible plan for bringing their idea to market, usually presented in a more measured way. The idea itself was invariably feasible — a workable solution of novelty within existing parameters. The mixed group was often more interesting, more considered and a combination of greater novelty and greater depth of detail.

On around three quarters of these occasions, the panel awarded the diverse team the 'prize' (a box of chocolates) for best idea. They seemed to combine greater breadth of novelty, with more detail, and somehow generated trust in their capacity to deliver.

When a diverse team sets out, with prior learning around A-I, and an intent to use the best of their mixed styles, they increase the odds of success.

The Leader and the Problem-solving Process

Leaders are likely to have two challenges regarding the management of diversity. The first is in accessing enough of it. Where the immediate team is too narrow in range of thinking, something extra needs to be brought in.

However, the more common challenge is for leaders is to learn the skills to maximise the presence of diversity. It is not new thinking to state that the role of the leader is to leverage effectively the available diversity to match the complexity of problems faced. While they'll often have a contribution to make around the problems being discussed, experience says that, as leaders become more senior, so their role shifts to being a 'conductor' of the diverse talents available.

In the *bridger* role, a person increases cohesion within the team by bringing together people with diverse styles. This takes some skill. The work is to educate people about the differences in the team, and the potential value of that, in relation to the work they face. This sounds matter-of-fact, but an effective bridger is likely to have these attributes:

- The bridger's own KAI score will most likely be intermediate in the range of the group. (The further to the extremes is the bridger's score, the more coping effort is required, and motive to fuel it.)
- A willingness to take the role.
- It also helps to have a set of skills around process facilitation and chairing groups.
- Finally, it also helps if the bridger has the genuine acceptance of others.

Research Support for Adaption-innovation Theory

More than 300 academic articles and over 100 theses have reviewed, applied and tested A-I theory. Criticisms of the work include some researchers finding correlations between individuals' KAI scores and measures of creative ability. They argue that style and level of creativity are not quite independent.[6,7] There is also too little written about the pragmatic transfer of the theory into practice. This book aims to help in that direction. Practitioners sometimes find his use of the term 'innovator' to be unhelpful, since the term is in such common, widespread use, and it requires open-mindedness to reset one's meaning of the term.

Other research studies have brought insights through Kirton's work. Buttner and Gryskiewicz found that entrepreneurs had a more innovative preference than did managers in larger US organisations.[8] Presumably the 'looser' structure of the work attracted them. More adaptive entrepreneurs tend to spend more time administering ongoing activities of the firm. While the more innovative were more attracted to the startup situation, the failure rate was higher among them. Writing a structured business plan is energy consuming for the more innovative, and many did not do it. A main cause of failure for the more adaptive minded was too strong a focus on the existing business plan arrangements, without regard for a changing market place.

Perhaps, the more innovative are attracted to the looseness of initiation, but, once the start-up phase is successful and more systematic, structure and process efficiency is required, and a more adaptive approach is needed. As Kirton himself summarises:

> This suggests that the complex, continuous problem is a moving target, in which an individual may be cognitively ideally suited to some phases, but, as a result of successful resolution, may not be as well suited to the succeeding phases that emerge later.[3] (p. 75)

Looking at the role of design thinking, Rieple concluded that designers are typically able to produce an abundance of ideas, some outside the organisations's current paradigm.[9] In other words, designers are likely to bring a more innovative preference. They are also likely to experience frustration when they encounter different occupational groups, who are likely to be more adaptive. Yet, both are needed for the successful fruition of ideas. She advocates collaboration and productive coping strategies as both parties need each other.[9]

With regard to role attractiveness, Tullett looked at a sample of 203 in-role managers of multiple projects and found them to have a mean KAI preference of 108, compared to a sample of 559 managers who averaged 98. Why did the work attract those with a more innovative preference? Tullett described the nature of the work involving cross-functional working, with simultaneous management of multiple projects, of different sizes. There is 'plate-spinning' happening here, and the need to shift, fluidly, from one piece of work to another, as well as across different project sponsors. Also, the nature of project work itself involves change. It is not documented how radical was the nature of change in this study, but the work would be more likely to attract those who prefer a less-structured work life.[10]

Previde and Rotondi looked at a case study of an Italian healthcare organisation. Their work focused on how the senior team varied the balance of A-I in the team, over the lifetime of the work. In the initial stages of the project, the team was more skewed to an innovation tendency. As implementation was required, so the team grew and recruited a balance of people with more of an adaption orientation. In the researchers' view, the management and application of diversity was guided by the importance of matching it to the complexity of the wider environment and its challenges.

> In this case, team changes in the composition of the cognitive profile of the team occurred in a way that produced cognitive outputs which were coherent with the environmental needs and team aims.[11]
> (p. 133)

In their efforts to help educate engineering students about the ideation process, Yilmaz *et al.* looked at how KAI style influences idea development. They asked students to produce a shortlist of sketched, design ideas to overcome the problem of providing effective personal transportation on snow. Skis and snowboards require skill to use, and don't run easily uphill. How might we design ways of helping individuals, without skills in skiing or snowboarding, to transport themselves on snow? In line with the theory they found that:

> These cases indicated a potential difference in that students who are more innovative on the KAI spectrum would generate solutions that venture away from familiar solutions compared to students who are more adaptive on the KAI spectrum. However, more adaptive students seemed to focus on more practical, less risky solutions with a promise of immediate efficiency.[12] (p. 12)

Summarising Adaption-innovation Differences

By now, you may have some insights into your preferred problem-solving style. Table 6.1 is adapted from the KAI profile feedback booklet and added to, in the light of our experience in working with A-I theory. Read the summary and follow the steps after it, requiring you to think through the implications for yourself and your team.

Remember that people are neither adaptors nor innovators. The primary considerations are 'fit' with the requirements of the current problem, and with the social pressures resulting from the styles of the people with whom we work.

For perspective with the general population, a KAI score

- of less than 83 is more adaptive than around 75% of people. Anything in this 25% of the population can be termed a highly adaptive score;
- between 83 and 95 is more innovative than the 25% of strong adaptors and more innovative than 50% of the remaining population. Anything in this quartile is a moderately adaptive score;
- between 96 and 108 is more innovative than 50% of the population and more adaptive than the remaining 25%. This is a moderately innovative quartile;
- of more than 108 is more innovative than 75% of people. This is more innovative than 75% of the population and is a highly innovative quartile.

Table 6.1: Adaption–innovation characteristic differences

The more adaptive…	The more innovative…
Prefer their problem solving to be more structured.	Prefer their problem solving to be less structured.
Tend to approach problems within the existing frame of reference. Like the problem to be consensually and tightly agreed, within generally accepted constraints. Value group cohesion. The most important considerations are: early resolution of problems, limited disruption and immediately increased efficiency.	Tend to reject the generally accepted view of the problem, challenging existing approaches and methods, and redefining problems, differently to how they are customarily perceived. Their view of the problem may be hard to convey. They may be more concerned with long-term gains than with immediate efficiencies.
Are more likely to change the structure in order to bring about desirable change.	Are more likely to bring about change in order to change the structure.
In solution generating — they tend to produce a few novel ideas, which are aimed at improving 'doing things better'. They often have confidence in implementing these, regardless of size and complexity.	Can generate many ideas — radical and more incremental. They are more likely to produce solutions that are seen as being 'different' and change the existing system. They may find it hard to prioritise these and may not know which ones will 'pay off'.
Prefer work that provides a more structured situation. Will often try to incorporate emerging data or events into the existing structure, to make it more efficient.	Prefer work that is less structured, and with fewer rules to guide action. Will often try to use new data or events as opportunities for introducing new policies or structures, accepting the risk that goes with this.
In their working approach, they are more likely to note precedent, arrange data in orderly ways and search methodically for relevant information. Use their creativity to refine and improve the current approach, with speedier and lower-risk progress. If that is what is needed, their approach can be efficient.	They are more likely to pay less attention to the immediate structure enveloping the problem. They gain a wider overview by taking themselves outside the existing approach, and bringing insights from beyond the current boundaries, and breaking the paradigm. If that is what is needed, their approach can be efficient.

(*Continued*)

Table 6.1: (Continued)

The more adaptive...	The more innovative...
Use rules as efficient guidelines, rather than adhering to everyone. Bring people together, achieving consensus to bring about change. Modify the rules cautiously, achieving great changes gradually.	More likely to solve problems by bending, even breaking, the rules. Able to 'shake up' the current order, when sudden, radical change is required.
They provide value through supplying the pragmatic base of stability, order and continuity so that riskier ventures can be attempted. Tend to give more attention to matters within the system, and tend to become authority within the system. Masters of pragmatic approaches and knows 'what will work here and what won't'.	They give more attention to matters emerging from outside the system. They can often anticipate the trends that will change the way we work. They supply the break with the past and accepted approaches without which institutions can ossify.
A potential weakness is that they find it difficult to see the disadvantages of the current system and *stay with it* past the point where it can be saved by improvement. In times of *unexpected change, they may find it difficult to rearrange into new formations.*	A potential weakness is that they find it difficult to see the advantages of the current system. May want to *change the current system too fast* — when it still offers the promise of solving the problem. They may have difficulty in applying themselves with discipline to ongoing organisational work.
May need to learn strategies for generating more radicalism in their problem defining and solution generating - to match the usefulness of their insights. May also need to learn to tolerate unexpected challenge.	May need to learn strategies for ensuring their more radical ideas are also workable. May need to learn how to challenge others without offending, so that these challenges lead to dialogue not conflict.
Innovators may see adaptors as sound, conforming, reliable, unenterprising, wedded to the system and norms, inflexible and intolerant of ambiguity.	Adaptors may see innovators as risk takers, perhaps glamorous, sometimes abrasive and insensitive, impractical and as threatening the established system.

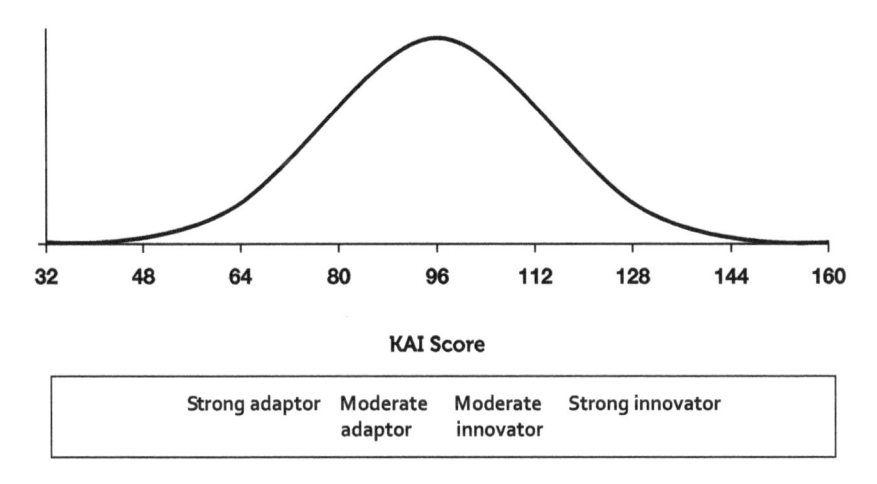

Figure 6.3: Estimating KAI preference

Best-guess your KAI score, and plot it on the continuum given in Figure 6.3.

So What? Reflections on Adaption-innovation Theory

Read the following section and consider the potential implications for you and your team members.

A. Work — What attracts and satisfies us?

Our problem-solving preference has an impact on the types of work to which we are attracted. People with a more adaptive preference like work where there is enough structure and routine and where improvements are needed. Most medium or large-sized organisations have well-established systems, processes, structures for ongoing functions, that need to be more efficient. Their very definition of the innovation challenge is likely to be contained within the context of the existing approach. And their solutions will make the existing approaches better, with lower risk, more likely lower cost, and well thought through pragmatic incrementalism. Strong and moderate adaptors tend to want to work within the established processes and 'fine-tune' them.

Most changes in medium to large organisations are of this sort, and, over time, this can equate to significant improvement. Examples include

Kaizen improvement cycles, most lean approaches and the marginal gains approach of, for example, the UK Cycling team.[13]

The great potential value of adaptive improvement is its inherent potential for making significant, additive change over less time, at low cost, with low risk to the organisation. The more adaptive tend to focus on improving internal organisational processes and structures, rather than anticipating the trends that will make the organisation change. The major blind spot comes in times of crisis when they may have trouble in perceiving that the current approach itself may be part of the problem. The stronger the person's adaptive preference, the more pronounced is this risk.

People with a more innovative preference seem to prefer more unstructured work where there is no prescribed way of doing things. Examples of work include new projects, pathfinder projects, the requirements for 'breakthrough' thinking, start-ups, work that is new to the organisation and has few rules. All of these may be attractive to people with the more innovative preference, specially since their attention is on precisely those (usually external) trends that will force organisational change. When they are in this well-matched zone of personal style and work demand, the more innovative can produce thinking that yields precisely those ideas that are most groundbreaking for organisations. This is the great potential value of the innovative style. However, as work makes progress, and is deemed successful, so comes the need for efficiency through structured process improvement. The more innovative may have trouble in applying themselves to more routine organisational demands. Through motivation they may be able to push themselves to cope, but, depending on opportunities, they may find quicker satisfaction through finding another unstructured piece of work.

Kirton's research has shown that differences in the degree of structure in different occupations does attract people with different KAI styles. For example, mean KAI scores around 80–90 (strong to moderate adaptor) have been found for Bank Managers, civil servants, production managers and maintenance engineers. Whereas in work with less structure, such as marketing, fashion buying and planning, KAI means were found of 104–110 (moderate to strong innovator).[14]

Reflective question: Knowing yourself, and having guessed your KAI style, what sorts of work do you find attractive and energising?

B. Coping with cognitive gaps, health and well-being

Your KAI problem-solving preference is not behaviour but is an influence on it. As we've heard, Kirton argues that our style preference does not change over our life, but our ability to cope and stretch away from our preference certainly does. Sometimes we have to stretch away from our preferred approach, because of the intrinsic nature of the work itself; situational demands, including the perception of threats and rewards; the needs of others, and more...

As we take on more responsibility, so our range of 'work' increases, and this is certainly true for team leadership.

With greater experience, we learn strategies to cope, and these become key to our effectiveness and well-being. Motivation is the raw fuel for driving our coping behaviour, enabling us to push ourselves beyond our figurative comfort zones to get work done. Though motivation, by itself, doesn't determine the coping strategies we use (see Table 6.2).

And the effectiveness of these coping strategies is key, because coping takes energy. The further we stretch away from our preference, and the longer the time, the more energy it takes and this rises exponentially.

Furthermore, experience tells us that, even with a moderate amount of pressure, if the energy from motive starts to wear out, people will tend to revert to their KAI style preference.

But we do learn successful coping strategies?

In the context of the innovation process, one way that people learn to cope is through learning specific thinking tools that are more or less structured. We explored the use of creativity tools in Chapter 4. People can and do learn to extend their zone of effective functioning for idea generation and development. The working method that one person takes as normal practice can sometimes be a revelation to another.

For example, the more adaptive can learn to use 'looser' thinking tools, often to enable more divergent thinking. Random and reverse brainstorming, and provocative pictures are examples of this. The more innovative can learn to use 'tighter' thinking tools, often to enable more convergent

Table 6.2: Adaption–innovation coping strategies

When work forces them to use less structure, the more adaptive may cope by...	When work forces them to use more structure, the more innovative may cope by...
Motivating themselves to move from agreed structures into riskier work territories they usually skilfully avoid.	Motivating themselves to survive and thrive in a successful group by mastering the rules and agree a consensus.
Using problem-solving techniques to stimulate more novel thinking. For example, more divergent, or less structured.	Using problem-solving techniques to stimulate more practical thinking.
Learning when and how to stimulate more debate for the good of the work.	Learning to challenging people in more socially acceptable ways, so that the challenge is 'heard' and discussed.
And, while being forced to stretch away from preference, finding other, more adaptive, work inside or outside the workplace, that suits their style and replenishes their energy. (Even when this increases their workload.)	And, while being forced to stretch away from preference, finding other, more innovative, work inside or outside the workplace, that suits their style and replenishes their energy. (Even when this increases their workload.)

thinking. The evaluation matrix and paired comparison analysis are examples here.

In my experience this is best done in short, purposeful bursts, assisted by a trained facilitator, who understands the 'rules and design' behind the use of these tools. This helps learners master the use of the tools. Such learning is often fun and can extend the range of an individual's range of effective practice.

When coping strategies fail to serve the individual in their context, our tiredness leaves us with less resource to stretch away from our preference. At times like this we will revert to our style preference, with all its pros and cons. We may procrastinate, avoiding the difficult work situation, be absent and sometimes get ill. If people don't find a sufficient coping strategy, they sometimes change job roles, within or outside the organisation.

When leaders are struggling to cope, their style preference will show to others, perhaps with the leader's frustrations and irritations.

At times like this, it can be helpful for someone to share some feedback with the leader on how they are affecting others. Whether they do so will depend on the trust in the relationship and the perceived risk of speaking frankly.

Story: Unsuccessful Leader Coping

This global oil and gas organisation, located in southern Europe, was facing challenging times. Energy prices were falling, global competition was increasing and environmental pressures were growing. The Managing Director (MD) had asked us to work with 200 of his staff and to train them in creative problem solving. He wanted to elicit more ideas from more people in the business, and to support them through training. This included the KAI. The MD's KAI score was 132 — more innovative than around 98% of people. He explained,

> Of course, I really value the work of adaptors. They bring stability, cohesion and reliability to our business. Without them we'd deliver nothing...

As we continued the work, and began to build relationships with the people, a different story emerged. Under the growing pressure, the MD was liable to give signs that what he really wanted was quicker, more radical change. People 'got the vibes' about this and they did not feel valued. This was communicated not through his words, but through his tone, impatience, body language and annoyance at change being both too slow and too incremental for his liking. Given that almost all people were more adaptive than the MD, they were keeping their heads down until the latest storm blew past.

The MD didn't know the messages he was sending out, as stress found him reverting to his preferred strongly innovative style. He didn't know the impact that these communication 'leaks' were having on people, so caught up was he in his desire for more radical change. And his direct reports weren't going to tell him because the risk was too high.

According to Boyatzis, we sense others' moods in milliseconds — before we know we have done so, and before we can think about and respond to them. Of course, our emotional responses are noticed by others.

> Our unconscious emotional states are arousing emotions in those with whom we interact before we or they know it. And it spreads from these interactions to others... The leader, because of his/her position of power, has a greater effect on others in a social or work environment. Being able to change your internal state might be one of the most powerful techniques you learn in becoming an effective leader– one who inspires others to learn, adapt and perform at their best.[15] (p. 2)

In the above case, people sensed frustration and annoyance from a highly innovative leader. They sensed these feelings and decided not to tell the leader about their concerns directly. Despite the leader's spoken words about the value of adaptors, his emotions revealed more to people than did his words.

(We didn't stay with the business long enough to see the final outcomes of this. While we were there, the effect of the above pattern was that organisational change progresses more slowly than the MD wanted.)

Reflective questions: What coping strategies do you tend to use? How effective are these? What else might you do?

C. Implications for leading teams for better problem solving

Your own fit with your work, and your ability to cope effectively are both important considerations for the sustainability of your efforts. However, your bigger role is to maximise the diversity potential of your team.

Experience shows that leaders do a better job with handling their team diversity once they have thought through the implications for themselves. For example, you have a preferred style of problem solving and this affects the 'problems' you perceive, define, are motivated to pursue and to avoid.

Being the leader, and with the power you possess, you really need to know about this, because your people may say they agree with you even when they don't. Knowing more about your strengths, blind spots and potential behaviour under pressure, you are better equipped to get the most from your team.

In synthesising the implications from A-I theory, and from training and coaching over 2,700 people with the KAI inventory, the following reflections may help:

- *Frame the conversation around a common goal*: As we've seen, it is a real challenge to ingrain innovation in the everyday work activities of people, and, more importantly, in a way that is genuinely meaningful to them. As leader, you have the power to frame conversations, and your problem-solving preference may affect the conversations you consider important. What energises you may not energise others! Your antennae may be pointing in the wrong direction. A more adaptive style will be more focused on improving internal organisational matters. A more innovative style will involve you in noticing external trends and dynamics that might bring change. Don't let your own filtering and biases reduce your team's agenda to what satisfies you. Involve others and get them to share what they consider important, are noticing and want to work on. Employ your self-awareness, with a dash of humility, in the service of a goal bigger than yourself. Involve your team in deciding what topics really matter so that there is a meaningful common goal for your team.
- *Bridging*: As a team leader you may think this is a natural role for you to take. It may not be. The further away from the group average is your KAI score, the more motivation and skill it will take for you to assume this bridger role, and to be accepted by others. In most teams, moderate adaptors and moderate innovators tend to make better bridgers, assuming these are in an intermediate position for the group they are serving. (Where the organisational agenda is becoming more radical, moderate innovators can be very effective. They often have a sympathy for more radical change, but temper it with an appreciation of the need to bring others along. They can be a natural change agents in large organisations that require a more fundamental re-upholstering.)

    Ask yourself whether you are the best bridger available. Accept that your more important role is to galvanise the diversity of others, rather than demonstrate your own problem-solving flair. You may find

it simpler to give someone else the bridger role, freeing you up to add different value.
- *Say why*: Leaders should say to their team, publicly and explicitly, why they need a range of thinking styles. That sounds cringingly simple, and yet…it's not said often enough and convincingly enough. Tell your people why you need the differences they possess.
- *Match styles to work demands*: If the work of your team is complex and requires a diversity of approaches over time, then you, as the leader, will need to optimise the diversity you have available. As the first option, use people's strengths, and match them with work that gives them opportunity to produce more adaptive or more innovative creativity — to fit their preference.
- *Match styles to different phases of work*: Your strategic change agenda should dictate the degree of solution radicalness needed. Some phases of work may require a more structured approach, others less so. However, you're still likely to need a spread of incremental and more radical ideas. Broadly, idea generation usually requires a more divergent, less-structured mindset. Whereas implementation is more of a social and political process, when you'll need senior leader attention, sponsorship and genuine support for your idea. The more adaptive generally think more about consensus, and the realities of enabling change given the detail of the actual processes, systems and structures we have in place right now. Consider workflow, and which stages will need more adaptive and more innovative efforts. Invite your people to contribute as the stages require.
- *Pairing with each other*: The simplest strategy for the effective use of diversity is the pair. People form pairings of difference all the time, working with people they trust and who give a different, and useful, point of view. Encourage the organic development of pairings.
- *Learning*: When your team members perceive that a work challenge requires a more deliberate use of diverse thinking styles, pairing might not be enough. They may need to work in larger groups. Consider taking them through an overview of A-I theory as a prelude to their work. Education can bring insight, and an understanding of the potential value of difference.

- *Everyone can be creative*: Remember that both adaptors and innovators have novel ideas. With their greater facility for producing many ideas, innovators may become associated with idea generation and adaptors may suffer by comparison. But novelty must be considered in specific contexts. Encourage both adaptors and innovators in their different styles of idea generation. You need all ranges of ideas. Read this story, as an illustration.

Story: A Fishy Tale…

(The origins of this story are a bit murky, and, no doubt, altered in the various retellings. But it illustrates a point.)

An organisation produced and sold fishtanks for a domestic market. They built the fishtanks from metal frames and glass, and mailed them, ready-built, through their long-term contracted distributor. The problem was that too many fishtanks broke en route. Too many customers received cracked or smashed products. The organisation was contracted to remain with the distributor, and could not change the materials or production method.

How did the organisation solve this problem of product waste, customer dissatisfaction and negative impact on profits? Please think about it and note down some potential solutions.

Most people think along the lines of: add packaging, change the distribution approach, help the consumer to build it themselves… The solution was around the packaging. They removed it! No packaging meant more visibility of the product and ensured that the distributors took more care in loading it. Greater care led to fewer breakages. This was an example of adaptive creativity because the structure of the approach remained the same. All that changed was a (very novel) amendment, within existing parameters, at minimal cost and time, and balanced risk, to produce an effective solution.

- *Reflective questions*: How well do you, as leader, tolerate approaches that are different to your own? How can you use KAI theory and practice to use diversity in teams more effectively?

Case 1: The Law Firm — More Structure Please

The context

This law firm had established a new team to set up online services as a channel for existing and new legal services. Which of their legal services could also be offered in digital format, complementing their face to face offerings?

The hope was that this blended offering would differentiate them in the marketplace and give them a strategic competitive advantage. To bring this about the team's role was to speak to key internal stakeholders, especially divisional directors, and to prioritise the development of e-business ideas from concept to implementation so that these delivered commercial value.

The challenges

When I walked into the team's main office room, I saw walls covered in flipchart paper and post-it notes. Everywhere I looked showed evidence of new and different thoughts. There was less evidence of focus.

As I talked with the team leader I learnt more about their work challenges. The team of five people had been talking with their divisional directors, who were the service 'owners' for specific legal offerings. As they learnt about these services and weighed up whether they'd be appropriate for offering through their online channel, their usual response was to say: 'Yes, we could do that...' The team members genuinely saw the possibilities and were excited about what they might achieve.

However, given their slim resources and the growing expectations within the business, the team needed to consider how they would make decisions about prioritising and implementation. They'd been quick to see the potential for providing a new way to market for these services. And now their internal customers expected them to deliver and to see results.

The team was nine months into the project and, so far, had delivered nothing. Pressures were growing, their reputation was beginning to diminish and team morale was falling.

Table 6.3: Ebusiness team KAI results

Team	Mean score	Range	Leader score
Ebusiness team ($n = 5$)	116	104–131	131

What had happened here? The five-team members completed the Kirton A-I questionnaire and the results were striking (see Table 6.3).

The team had responded to an internal advertisement for this new project, written along the following lines:

> Applications are welcomed for an exciting new, strategic project. Our business wants to develop an online presence and be at the leading edge of service development in our industry. This innovative project will build our capacity to deliver our services through an online presence, as well as our more traditional...

The advertisement had unwittingly attracted people with a more innovative problem-solving preference. The mean score of the team was itself highly innovative. Importantly, the leader's KAI score was the most innovative of all.

We reviewed the scores and the implications with the whole team. People quickly grasped what was happening. The team had started with a strong sense of excitement, had generated many possibilities very quickly, but was now struggling to use sufficient structure to focus its efforts. They needed more adaptive behaviour.

The leader had several insights. First, he understood more clearly the critical value of adaptive behaviour, as part of the diversity that the team needed. He discussed this publicly with his team. He saw that they needed more process and administrative control to help them prioritise the development of potential ideas. Without this focus, the team would risk continuing with ever more divergent thinking.

Second, he understood that work could be allocated more productively to fit people's KAI preference. In the following months he pursued an approach of maximising strengths, giving more adaptive work to people with more adaptive preference, and more exploratory work for those with a more innovative preference. This improved both job satisfaction and work productivity and lowered stress levels.

Third, he improved his awareness of which team members had learnt effective coping strategies that gave them more 'bandwidth' for behaviour. When coping was needed, he supported these people in their coping efforts, to help achieve team goals.

Finally, immediately after this intervention the team was soon to recruit two people. The KAI is not a selection tool, but its insights can be used to frame questions and seek people with a more (or less) structured approach to problem solving. In the next two months, the team recruited a junior solicitor and an administrator. Both of these provided a more structured approach, giving the team improved breadth and balance.

Nine months later, I spoke with the team leader and he told me that they were now offering legal services online. One of them — an employment law training package — was already selling well. The team's internal reputation was much improved and so was their external market profile. They were gaining access to business development opportunities, winning new clients and new revenue.

Case Review

Many things contributed to this success, including politically aware stakeholder management and sheer persistence in seeking sales opportunities. A-I theory gave the team a framework for understanding the strengths and weaknesses of the team as a whole. It also gave them validation of their hunches — that they needed more structure in their approach. The specific data and insights from the KAI gave them the confidence to diagnose their next steps, and to focus their energies.

This change in approach to the process of team innovation was key to starting a virtuous spiral of productivity, improved morale, reduced stress, greater optimism and, in time, this contributed to tangible results.

Case 2: An Effective Pairing

Background

Ted is the Speciality Lead for the emergency department of a large hospital trust in the South of England. The department has around

300 staff (a mix of consultants, junior doctors, nurses and allied staff and serves around 95,000 patients per year).

He had little formal leadership development before taking a clinical leadership role:

> I trained for 15–20 years, to be an emergency medicine consultant, with no leadership training whatsoever. Everything I did was instinctive, and a feeling of common sense. At the start I was flying by the seat of my pants. In high-level meetings, with high-level people, just trying to do what I thought was right.

He attended an internal leadership development session, run by the hospital's learning and development team. This looked at the difference between strategic and operational leadership. Ted was excited and enthused after this, thinking there were things to learn, to do his job better. He applied for, and won, a place on a regional healthcare leadership development programme.

On the programme, Ted completed the A-I profile. His profile score of 82, placed him as a strong adaptor — more adaptive than around 75% of the population.

Rob: Your profile came out as being pretty strongly adaptive. When you got those results, what did it mean to you?

Ted: It made me laugh. Because, reflecting on what I know now, it showed me what I know, which is that I work within boundaries. If I don't have boundaries I find it quite scary and quite stressful. On a personal level, I felt that this is not necessarily a weakness. That's who I am and that's all right. If I work within constraints, it's where I'm most comfortable.

Rob: And do you mean that you, therefore, try to find those boundaries, in order to work within them?

Ted: Yes, if I don't have those boundaries, I don't know where to start. I have to have a constraint and a set of rules, to do the best within those boundaries. If I know what the limits are, it helps me come up with the solutions and move things forward.

Rob: And you laughed because?

Ted: Because I saw how much I am a conformist. Within the room at the leadership programme, it was fascinating to see the 'innovators' were the ones who challenged me most, I was most irritated by, and I couldn't understand their point of view. And sometimes I was quite dismissive of how they approached problems or answers, because I felt it wasn't what we were being asked, they weren't answering the questions within (what I thought was) the framework that we were expected to answer.

If I extrapolate that to my work… I sometimes got short tempered by a couple of team members, because I felt they didn't listen to the question we had to solve. They would go off on tangents; they look from a different point of view and try to sort things beyond our control.

I recognised that I see them as innovators and that they have huge strengths in their own way. I need to stop being frustrated and let them go with it. They know I get irritated when I feel we are straying from what is our problem to solve into what I perceive to be out of our control.

Problem description and idea development

The problem we were trying to sort was patient flow in, through and out of our department. We were trying to keep our department safe for patients. I was trying to sort it out and do the best within our walls. The problems are recurrent: there aren't enough beds. The fundamental thing is that our door is always open. We have to keep absorbing that workload. If we can't get people out the other end, then our walls expand and we have to deal with that.

At the time, we decided where patients would go after our department. People wait in our department until the in-patient ward says: we have a space, and we let them in. That was the standard.

My colleague, Jo, said: Why can't we get every single ward to take one extra patient? Then we're spreading the risk and sharing the load, and making it better for all the patients. The evidence is that patients do better in that situation, rather than queuing in one single location.

Jo was saying we've got to sort this problem 'out there'. She was broadening the problem. I was saying: we've got to control what we want to do — keeping the problem within the boundaries of our department. She argued: we need to get the wards to recognise this is a shared problem and they are best placed to help with the solution. For example, if another ward has 20 beds and has to deal with 21 patients, they will know best which patients they can discharge home to free up the bed for that additional patient. That's a massive sea change. There was great resistance to it, because it's sharing the ownership of the problem more widely.

At the start I was thinking: 'yes of course they should be doing it but it's too big — they're not going to do it...'

She took this idea and started talking to more people in the hospital — not taking no for an answer. And people started to listen to her. She was using her time and energy and a massive amount of discretionary effort. I realised that she was making headway with her idea and I needed to support her.

How Ted supported the new idea

Ted: Jo can get bogged down in details; I'm probably better at being eloquent about the answer, reassuring people, bringing people with us. We'd go to meetings and I'd give it the more sanitised version. I reassured others and I gave Jo the backing and confidence.

Some people strongly resisted this change, and occasionally were antagonised by the idea. But, it had to be done — that challenging role and being thick skinned around it. So, then I would try and support her and smooth the paths around her.

Also, I gave her formal work time to develop the idea and fought for her to get paid for her efforts. She'd gone over and above what was expected. She felt uncomfortable about getting paid, whereas I felt very comfortable about it. My role was to say: she's done a fantastic job and she needs to get recognised for this. I was comfortable fighting on her behalf.

Rob: What's been the effect of the change?

Ted: Astonishing. We have routinely spread the risk. It is expected that that load is shared and this is embedded into policy. This winter, when headlines were about 'A&E is falling over...', colleagues are phoning me from around the region asking: How have you managed this? We were ahead of the game.

Rob: Knowing your (adaptive) style, what could you do that she couldn't?

Ted: We got to this place because she achieved it. She, singularly, has made the biggest difference over patient flow in the hospital, and I am in awe. I could be the acceptable face of the emergency department. The pragmatist, seeing it from all sides. I'm better at being the external-looking, political face of the department.

Rob: To me it sounds like you're belittling your role in it. Would she have got the change through without you?

Ted: Yes, but she wouldn't have got paid. She appreciated the support I gave her.

Rob: And when you said you needed to stop being frustrated, how have you done that?

Ted: I'm not an innovator but I try and help people who are innovators. It's nice for me to know that someone is different and can run away with something, (an idea), and it's not a weakness in me. That someone can do it and I can't. That's the most important thing I learnt — that my weaknesses don't mean I'm a bad leader — I just need to play to my strengths and that's OK.

Case Review

Ted's growing self-awareness, acceptance of his own problem-solving style, and attendant strengths and limitations, is neatly illustrated here. And, aside from his increasing awareness, there is clear evidence of applying his learning to extend his effective problem-solving range. The real aim of A-I theory is to broaden our effective problem-solving scope, whether working alone or collaboratively.

Jo expanded the definition of the problem beyond the physical and cultural boundaries of the A&E department, whereas Ted was still thinking within it. This is a classic difference between the looser, less structured approach of Jo, and the tighter, more structured one of a strong adaptor.

Jo was the first to see the potential for her idea. Initially, Ted was unconvinced. Once the idea started to gather interest from people, Ted realised he needed to change his thinking. He then provides support for Jo and her idea, within the existing social, political and emotional structures of the hospital. Specifically,

- he gave support in formal, public meetings, attended by him, Jo and people from other wards. In these meetings, Ted was able to reassure people, through his strong emotional intelligence, and his demonstrable understanding of the working of the hospital. If Ted thinks it can work, it reassures people;
- the idea brought resistance. Jo becomes the 'bad guy' and Ted recognises this. He also understands that this degree of challenge is necessary for the success of the idea. He ensures that the idea is aired publicly, and he supports and encourages Jo;
- he gives Jo formal time to develop her idea;
- finally, he fights successfully for Jo to receive pay that reflects the extra time she put into developing his idea.

As a strong adaptor, Ted understands the workings of the various, existing structures of her work environment. Without these formal settings, with people being prepared to listen to the idea, and consider its strengths, there might have been a less happy outcome, and certainly a more 'bumpy' ride.

Senior level, strong adaptors typically understand the social, political and emotional structures within an organisation. They are often able to support an idea through these necessary steps, beyond idea generation and into the more social and political world of idea implementation. Because of their preference for high structure, they also think hard about social structures like agreeing consensus in key, formal meetings.

Ted is a modest leader, describing a case of 'live' learning, with a frank illustration of a change in his own problem-solving approach. Without Jo, the idea would not have been publicly aired or progressed. Ted has clearly enabled the progress of the idea through the internal organisational decision-making processes. What's more clear is that the approach has become part of the policy and way of working of the trust. A radical approach has become part of the prevailing, current structure. Strong, smart adaptors can sell radicalism when they are convinced.

It helped that Ted has a good degree of emotional intelligence — enough to note the early worries of others, allay them, and maintain good working relationships. This is not an aspect of A-I theory. Adaptors are not necessarily more adept at this than innovators. It just happens that Ted has this quality and used it well.

Case 3: Fitting People to the Work

Background

Donna is the head of a business unit for this global business services organisation. Her business supports customers across the UK. Donna is also a strong innovator. In Kirton's terms, she is in that quartile of most innovative across the general population. I had been coaching Donna through a transition stage of her leadership role, over a 12-month period. During this time, we brought together her team of direct reports, and she and they completed the KAI inventory. The story below describes that event, and the strategic context in which Donna was attempting to introducing change across her business.

Rob: What was the strategic context that meant that change and more ideas were needed?

Donna: From a UK-wide perspective, and global, we had identified a strategic need to diversify into different markets, where we could take our existing solutions. And the opportunities were vast in the SME market. It was a strategic initiative for growth. And there were changes in the market, generally, towards a more technology-enabled world. We had already seen significant growth and were profitable, but we had to change to achieve a vision of aspirational growth and quadrupling our business in a very short time.

And I was struggling to bring the team with me. I always felt that I was running ahead of them, and I was finding that frustrating.

Rob: Yes, I remember that: it felt like there was a gap growing between your vision and their daily practice.

Donna: Yes, we talked frequently at our planning and strategy meetings around the future and where we needed to get to. To me, it felt like it was a need-to-do,

Table 6.4: SME business team KAI results

Team	Mean score	Range	Leader score
SME business team (*n* = 7)	98	82–123	120

rather than something we were doing. We'd allocate tasks, but it still felt like they'd stare at me, a bit blankly. I was concerned that it was about my communication: Am I getting this across well enough? Were they excited? Did they 'get' it? When I tested that with them, they said, yes, they were excited, we can see where the business is going to grow. But the reality of getting there was a real challenge.

Rob: So, your developing feeling was that there was something of a gap growing between you and them. In 2016, we asked the team to complete the KAI questionnaire, then we met them, face to face, and shared the results. There was a strong clustering at the more adaptive end, with you and another team member at the high innovator end (see Table 6.4).

Donna: The gap between me and most of them was significant. It was an eye-opening moment. Thinking about it in that way made sense straight away. What was interesting about it was that they were grouped together closely, with one of them being nearer to the mid-point. I realised I was getting these people to make a leap. I was saying 'just make the change now and we'll deal later with the fallout'. And they didn't see that could possibly be achieved.

Rob: And, since then, what kind of learning have you had?

Donna. That didn't stop us needing to change our business, but I was in a situation where people were focusing on the day-to-day work, that they had to do. And they were comfortable in that. Strategically, we were also involved in some business acquisitions which distracted us, temporarily, from our organic growth strategy. In 2016, we didn't achieve the things we needed to — from the perspective of jumping forward as much as we wanted. The changes were incremental. As an example, we felt that we needed to restructure our business to be focused on client delivery, rather than product delivery. For me, that doesn't feel like a massive change. But, by the end of 2016, we'd made some steps, but we hadn't restructured.

But, the knowledge of the styles of people I had in the team meant I could live with that. We were dealing with the acquisitions and those people could deliver what they needed to, in their way, with existing clients. And we needed to focus on the business. So, strategically, we still had our vision, but we had an unexpected breathing space, allowing people to make incremental changes, gradually moving towards our goal. But we weren't ripping everything up and starting again.

Rob. Was it frustrating for you — did you have to show some self-management?

Donna. Oh yes! My frustrations would come out as: What am I doing wrong here? I'd still get blank looks when I was talking about the vision. I'd say to myself: 'We've been through this many times now, is it how I'm communicating it?' But then I'd rethink and say to myself: 'hold on — for these guys, we are making change. Which is different to my view of what change really means.' And being able to reflect on the folks in the team, made me able to accept that we were OK for now.

But what was interesting through that period was that, aside from my immediate team, others in our business would say: you talk about change but nothing's changing; while other people would say: it's all change! So, for my direct reports — if they're at the more adaptive end of the continuum — their teams are a mix of people — some of them are fine with it but others are frustrated by it.

For me, that was difficult to manage as the leader of a business, when I've stood up and said: these are the changes coming and they're exciting. The last thing you want is to lose those people from the business, because you need to retain a spread of styles across the team.

Rob: So, with all these thoughts going on, your strategic need was still present. Bringing us up to date, what have you done to meet your more strategic marketplace needs?

Donna: Two things. Alongside me, at the innovative end, was our sales manager. But where we needed most change was in client servicing, where the more adaptive people were located. We needed more of a mix in there, but also someone who didn't get as frustrated as I do, or could introduce change at an easier pace, as sometimes I'll rush ahead in my thinking.

So, this is learning about myself. It's all very well me having a vision and leaping off down that road, but maybe I'm not the right person to always bring that team with me. Communicating the vision and strategy, yes, but I'm not necessarily the right person to bring them with me.

I recruited someone into the client services part of the business. We pitched it as: your job is 'to deliver a brilliant client-service experience'. Not: 'to deliver loads of change'. V joined the business early in 2017, with the role of making sure our service proposition delivered brilliant client experience; engaging and bringing our people with us; and developing our people so that they were able to deliver the service.

So, those things are happening, but with a differently worded objective: focusing it on customers — which they're more comfortable with — rather than focused on change *per se*. And V can spend more time with them, than I could. Including those who want faster change and have previously been frustrated. She's brought them in to contribute. And that has really helped.

Rob: So, part of your learning was to take a step back…

Donna. And that my frustrations would show. I'd say V fits more at the middle of the KAI range. She is focused on bringing people with her and gets less frustrated than me.

Meanwhile, my role has expanded and we needed to broaden the experience we had in the team on this sort of programme.

That was the first change we made. The other thing we've done is to have clearer vision on the transformation projects we need to implement in order to get there. I've recruited a transformation lead, to help us get where we need; help V with client services; digitally enable our business and help with the integration with our acquisitions.

We're going into a very significant period of change. As we talk about 2018, looking out to the vision, with those more adaptive people looking after our existing client book, we're being clear with those folks in that their role is to keep our ship stable. That's what they like. And they will get involved in other changes happening, but without the pressure of telling them: you have to deliver this change. The message will be: you don't need to worry about this because V has your backs here around client delivery; C has your backs on the sales side, and the new person — M — will bring both together with plans that progress key projects.

Rob: It sounds like you're saying that your more adaptive team leaders are more suited to the incremental change and the more radical and transformational change has new people and structures to enable it to happen.

Donna: Yes, and in a resource-tight business, where we can't bring in a new team to do this work, it means we need people focused on running the business. I learnt that the more adaptive people are good at managing people, workloads, and making sure that clients are renewed and reviewed: our traditional business. With that at the core, it gives us a platform of stability to both transform the business and make sure we're still delivering what we need.

Rob: It sounds like you've had to think differently about how to bring in the radical change?

Donna: It was naïve on my part. I think I'd just assumed that anyone can implement change if they have a plan. I thought: we have a plan — we'd drawn it up together. I hadn't taken into account that their thinking was different to mine. Now I think I was putting the wrong pressure on them: I was expecting them to hear me and deliver it. And to know how to. It was very unfair of me — to expect them to be able to do that.

Rob: And there's a limit to how much they can stretch.

Donna: Yes, though, in time, that may change as they move through the process and learn from others who've done this before. I guess the point is that having a mix of different folks is needed. With a knowledge of who you've got — and the KAI work enables that — and then thinking about what is needed in a transformational role.

Rob: And, through this time, what has staff retention been?

Donna: Strong. We have the same people in the team. They've liked having V as part of the team. She's calm! She's not running ahead all the time. With me, they'd be thinking: I'm not sure what she's talking about. And she's excited about it. Which meant they'd rather sit there silently than dampen my mood.

These experiences made me realise that, in order to grow our business; I need other people who can focus on running the business, and see the vision, and I can't do all of that.

Case Review

Donna is demonstrating a number of things here. She shows self-awareness, as she recognises her frustrations with the perceived lack of progress, and her wish to get involved in more of the transformational work.

She also demonstrates self-management and adaptability, recognising that she doesn't want her frustration to affect the team negatively. She reflects on what constitutes appropriate progress, and recalibrates her thinking.

She also shows empathy, noting how her team may feel with her expressed vision and excitement. They don't want to seem 'negative' by asking her questions that may slow down the pace of change.

Her growing awareness of the situation leads her to implement a series of changes, including

- fitting people to their preferred work, and a rate of change that suits them. She appreciates that adaptors fit more readily to the improvement of 'core' work delivery;
- she designs herself a new, more appropriate role, where she is more of an architect of change and less involved in the operational, day-to-day delivery;
- she recruits a more natural 'bridger' — V — to enable change and get buy-in from a wide range of people;
- she reframes the work challenge, and focuses the team on purposeful client-centric excellence, rather than a drive for introducing change for its own sake;
- she also acknowledges and addresses the frustrations of the more innovative people in her wider team;
- finally, she addresses the need for engagement and people retention. By building more in-depth capability, with people connected more with work that suits them, the unit is progressing more steadily with change, levels of stress are more manageable, and staff turnover levels are healthy.

Chapter Review — Practical Learning on Optimising Cognitive Diversity

In all three cases above, there was a tipping point, where the leaders involved perceived Problem A (the work challenge itself) being affected by problem B (the way in which people in the team were working together on the problem).

Another challenge, common to all three cases, was that of effective coping behaviour. In different ways, each leader was sufficiently aware that work wasn't going well enough. And he or she was sufficiently open to invite team members to consider alternatives.

This self-awareness and awareness of impact on others seems to be a critical point in using diversity well. We have seen other examples of teams where diversity remains a latent resource, unused because there is insufficient trust or psychological safety felt by team members.

Leaders learn a number of key points with A-I theory and practice. First, they learn about the strengths and limitations of their own style. This insight can be very useful, when combined with the mindset of an interdependent leader. Such leaders think unconsciously and consciously about mutuality. They know that they have value to offer, and so do others. And they seek, without their ego overwhelming the situation, to deploy the best of both.

Leaders also learn to harness difference around a common, purposeful goal. Donna changed the purpose away from pursuing change, *per se*, to one of serving their SME customers. Leaders who establish a meaningful, shared purpose find that thinking-style differences become an asset, in the service of the work.

The value to be gained from diversity also enables leaders to take some steps into the unknown. Ted appreciated the sheer energy and perseverance of Jo and took the risk of encouraging unusual action. He broadened the boundaries of what would normally be considered, and in doing so built the team's capacity for exploring novel solutions in a high-pressure situation.

And, when the leader is considering how their own style impacts on the climate of the team, for better or worse, they are simultaneously thinking about how to improve climate, for example, through connecting people to meaningful challenges, and allow for appropriate risk taking.

Finally, on a more emotional level, leaders should be aware of how they communicate and what impact this has. When we need novel thinking, outcomes are, by definition, unpredictable. Leaders may send messages that betray their own anxieties. They may also send signs that reveal their own preference for more incremental or more radical change. We have seen senior leaders switch off the motivation of their workforce by sending signals that reveal what they value. And what they don't. And 'what' they don't value soon becomes interpreted as 'who' they don't value!

Senior leaders should educate themselves about their own innovation preferences and adjust accordingly. A-I theory can be a pragmatic way of doing this. Using it with your team will tell you what spread of thinking styles you can call upon to face a given challenge.

References

1. Kirton, M. J. (1961). *Management Initiatives*. London: Acton Society Trust.
2. Kirton, M. J. (1989). *Adaptors and Innovators: Styles of Creativity and Problem Solving*. London: Routledge.
3. Kirton, M. J. (2003). *Adaption and Innovation in the Context of Diversity and Change*. London: Routledge.
4. Publications and current work using adaption-innovation theory. Kai Centre (2018). Available at: https://kaicentre.com/kai-publication-list-0817.pdf (Accessed on 31/03/2018).
5. Kurtzberg, T. R. (2005). "Feeling Creative, Being Creative: An Empirical Study of Diversity and Creativity in Teams." *Creativity Research Journal* 17(1): 51–65.
6. Torrance, E. P. and Yun Horng, R. (1980). "Creativity and Style of Learning and Thinking Characteristics of Adaptors and Innovators." *The Creative Child and Adult Quarterly* 5: 80–85.
7. Goldsmith, R. E. and Matherly, T. A. (1987). "Adaption-innovation and Creativity: A Replication and Extension." *British Journal of Social Psychology* 26: 79–82.
8. Buttner, E. H. and Gryskiewicz, N. (1993). "Entrepreneurs' Problem Solving Styles: An Empirical Study Using the Kirton Adaption/Innovation Theory." *Journal of Small Business Management* 31(1): 22–31.
9. Rieple, A. (2004). "Understanding Why Your Design Ideas get Blocked." *Design Management Review* 15(1): 36–42.
10. Tullett, A. D. (1996). "The Thinking Style of the Managers of Multiple Projects: Implications for Problem Solving When Managing Change." *International Journal of Project Management* 14(5): 281–287.
11. Previde, G. and Rotondi, P. (1996). "Leading and Managing Change through Adaptors and Innovators." *The Journal of Leadership Studies* 3(3): 120–134.
12. Yilmaz, S., Jablokow, K., Daly, S. R., Silk, E. M., and Berg, M. N. (2014). Investigating Impacts on the Ideation Flexibility of Engineers. Industrial Design Conference Presentations, Posters and Proceedings.
13. Syed, M. (2015). BBC. Available at: http://www.bbc.co.uk/news/magazine-34247629 (Accessed on 20/11/2017).
14. Kirton, M. J. (1985). Kirton Adaption Innovation Inventory feedback document. KAI distribution Centre, Chorleywood, UK.
15. Boyatzis, R. (2011). "Neuroscience and Leadership: The Promise of Insights." *Ivey Business Journal* 75(1).

Chapter 7

Sustaining Creativity Across Time and Scale

You can't use up creativity. The more you use, the more you have.

Maya Angelou[1]

The ABCD framework I've offered through this book, builds on the work of Rhodes and, I suggest, offers a pragmatic way of connecting sound creativity principles with everyday work challenges, assisted by the catalysing effect of mature leadership.

The perceived relevance for people is important. Given our capacity for reifying innovation — as discussed in Chapter 1 — we risk hyping the topic and distancing people from a meaningful, everyday experience of it. In this book, I've tried to establish that a more grounded approach is possible, desirable and is actually happening. Individual leaders are learning and applying creativity principles, in order to deliver value to the people they serve. The focus of the learning has been on these leaders, because they are catalysts in their contexts, accelerating change around them, through their mindful dispersal of the power and resources they possess. The leaders as individuals are neither the sole means nor the endpoint. But they still have a crucial role, acting as effective conduits, enabling and empowering others to do purposeful work.

However, one of the limitations of case studies is that they decontextualise. They capture stories of people, and frame them within time and character boundaries, in order to make a point. We may wonder: What happened before, and after? And with the types of challenges we're discussing — ones which need the imagination of groups, because simple solutions don't exist — one solution often creates another challenging set of circumstances. A characteristic of so-called wicked problems is their resistance to resolution. We produce good-enough solutions, for now, while being open to apprehending a new, emerging set of system dynamics which will need a different response.

In the UK health sector, the annual spend on upfront research and development in 2014–2015 was £1.2 billion. Whereas the approximate annual spend, from 2013 to 2018, to support adoption and spread of innovation, through their regional academic health sciences networks, was only £52 million. By pound investment, the sector is supporting initial idea development over their wider adoption by a factor of 24.[2]

When the same problems are present in multiple locations, but good solutions can't be spread, they get reinvented, in slightly different ways, to fit local contexts, but reinvented nonetheless. One of the consequences for people's goodwill is that work can feel like the proverbial hamster wheel. Improvements must be created from scratch, while the wheel itself is fixed in place. Energy replenishment becomes critical, otherwise people tire and switch-off.

All of which raises the matter of the need for sustainability. In particular, how to sustain creative problem-solving over time, and at a scale that might cross organisational boundaries, to suit the nature of the challenge?

Case 1: The Radical Education Offering

Context

This case looks at the introduction, in 2013, of the 'BA Hons Business (Team Entrepreneurship)' programme to the University of the West of England (UWE). It is an example of the wider adoption of an existing solution. The Tiimiakatemia (Team Academy) approach was developed and pioneered at Jyväskylä University of Applied Sciences in Finland in 1993. By 2013, it had been adopted by a number of other Finnish universities, and in a number of other European countries, including the Netherlands, Hungary and in the Basque country, Spain.

UWE and Northumbria University were pioneers in applying the programme at the same time to the UK. Since then, three other UK universities have adopted it.

Professor Carol Jarvis is a colleague, and trained in various innovation tools and diagnostics. These include the SOQ climate measure, discussed in Chapter 5, and a wide range of Creative Problem-Solving tools, described in Chapter 6. She is also an experienced tutor in creativity, innovation and entrepreneurship.

There are some important aspects of the Team Entrepreneurship programme, worth describing at this point. Within the first few weeks of joining the programme, the students (known as 'team entrepreneurs') are put into team companies, designed to be as diverse as possible. Each team company has its own 'team coach' and they train in their team company twice a week, for the duration of their degree. Through the programme, the team entrepreneurs learn about the principles of business through *doing* entrepreneurship — sourcing, delivering and evaluating a range of projects, a number of which will go on to be businesses that continue post-graduation.

Through the programme, the emphasis is on learning rather than teaching. The team coach's role is to support team entrepreneurs in the learning journey, encourage them to act, reflect, learn and take further action. This practice-based approach gives educational primacy to this virtuous cycle of doing informing learning, which in turn informs doing. (Rather than the lecturer being the source of the knowledge.)

It is seen as an exemplar programme for UWE's 2020 strategy, which has a commitment to practice-led learning and teaching as a key theme. It has become a sustainable feature of the enterprise offerings at UWE. It has started its 5th intake of undergraduate students and has graduated two intakes. Two further accredited degree programmes have been introduced adopting similar methods — MSc Innovation and Applied Entrepreneurship and a BA Hons degree programme, called Sports Business and Entrepreneurship, co-created with Bristol City Community Trust and offered from the Ashton Gate Stadium. All of this has provided external validation that the programme 'works'.

The Interview

Carol: At the beginning, a couple of people, from a CIC called Akatemia, who had seen the model working in Finland and wanted to bring it to the UK, came to tell us about a programme, all based on collaborative learning in teams. They called it learning by doing. I was intrigued but I also thought: What's so different here? It didn't sound so different from my own experience.

Rob: But there was something intriguing?

Carol: Particularly as they talked about outcomes for the young people who'd been through the programme. Several months later, they came back and said, to a group of us: Would you like a learning expedition to Finland? I'd shown interest in this so was selected. It's always interesting to see how other places do things. It was a really smart decision on their part!

When we turned up, over 3–4 days, we met over a third of the cohort. And they were these amazing, resilient, thoughtful young people. It wasn't necessarily the knowledge they had, it was more about their behaviours and their way of engaging with, and thinking about, work. They'd been running their own team companies. By the time they were graduating they looked more like someone at the end of a good grad development programme in an organisation.

So, we looked at the contextual differences. In Finland, higher education is free and the school system is different. And both Finland and the Basque Country, where the approach had widest adoption, have more collectivist cultures than the UK. We were incrementally adopting an innovation from something already working in Finland, and elsewhere, to adapt it for a different context in the UK. But, for us, it was a completely radical innovation.

Rob: Do you mean in the UK or this university?

Carol: Both. There were significant challenges. There are cultural challenges around the way people in the UK think about what education means. And there were some institutional challenges. The university was very supportive, but nonetheless we were doing something that really challenged some established processes and procedures.

For example, the Team Entrepreneurship (TE) programme runs on a 36-week year, whereas the rest of the university, works to a shorter calendar. None of the timings of our programme fitted with the university field and award boards, which is where marks are confirmed and formalised. You can't graduate without sign-off from Award Board, for example! We were asked: Can you bring their assignments forward? We thought: if we want them thinking about running a business, you don't want team entrepreneurs disappearing in May and coming back in September. That wouldn't happen in a business.

It was an example of a really important piece of learning for me: it's the little things that really catch you out.

Rob: And when you brought the programme back to UWE, were you now in a formal leadership role?

Carol: I had to report back to faculty executive on whether we should do it. And they took the bold decision to do it. I was given a role to lead on the programme development and how to train up people who were already working here.

There is a quite structured process to launch a new programme. It's very rule-bound. There are lots of external standards we have to meet, which make assumptions about specific types of knowledge. Whereas ours is practice-led and is about learning. These come from all sorts of levels, some imposed by the external QAA (assurance board), some by the institution.

There was a lot of moulding things: to meet these standards, and also to keep true to the spirit of the programme — which is what allows us to achieve our purpose. And at the same time, recognising that we wouldn't get through an approval process, if people couldn't see how it fitted in our system. And we needed to get it through the system to be able to offer the programme.

Rob: How did you handle this tension of maintaining focus on purpose and maintaining the required standards?

Carol: There was somebody on the Programme Design Group (PDG) Committee. He was really sceptical and also intrigued. And I worked with him as a critical friend. Several times, between each PDG meeting, I'd go back to him and ask: 'What's wrong with this?' I specifically said to him, 'Don't be nice to me. Provoke and ask me the right questions'. All of which made me think about what to do in response.

The measure of success of this approach was that our proposal went through with no conditions for change, and several examples cited of good practice for being used elsewhere. It saved months of the project development work, ensured the programme design was robust and reduced my stress levels significantly. It also meant when the programme, (and sometimes me at a personal level), was challenged in a public forum I had an effective response.

Rob: What were the challenges as you moved towards implementation?

Carol: Although we knew this was radically different and I had the support of senior managers, there was no recognition of how it would challenge us.

The challenges came from systemic things hidden within the organisation, which you don't see until you come to them. I learnt to get and maintain the support from key people in the wider organisation.

The implementation wouldn't have happened without the support of those people. I was thoughtful about when I hit barriers as to when and how I involved some of those key influencers. Not to wear them out by running back to them every time something happened. But also recognising, in a hierarchical organisation like, this people would listen differently to someone at a senior level.

Rob: And do you think that the more radical the change, the more that senior support is needed?

Carol: Absolutely. It was really important that they trusted me. And really important they were committed to the idea. I sometimes wished we were going through that learning curve in a less public way. But, if you asked me: Would it have happened without their support? No.

Because there'd have been too many of those little obstructions that we couldn't anticipate. It would have made me give up at some point. I wouldn't have had the time or level of influence. But, a 3-line, supportive email from the Dean of your Faculty opens doors.

So, use those relationships wisely. You know me, I'm quite a relational person. It's also about developing relationships with people in administrative roles and other bits of the university, so that when you go and ask them something that doesn't fit with what they normally do, they're inclined to work with you, rather than just say they can't do it.

The nature of the work was very emergent but the mindset was: there'll be challenges along the way, and we'll have to figure out how best to deal with them. For me, that's the absolutely critical thing, especially for something radically different. Nothing ever goes as you thought it would.

Rob: And looking back, to what extent was this a purposeful change, as opposed to an interesting experiment?

Carol: Philosophically, for me, I've never considered myself a teacher. I have a fundamental belief that we talk a lot about equipping student for jobs that don't even exist, and we can't know what they'll be. We have an education system which is moving further towards assessing knowledge, at a time when we should be promoting learning.

My purpose is to reintroduce the notion of learning. For me, you don't assess a graduate by looking at how much they know. You assess them by how effective they are at learning. For example, sourcing and valuing information, putting it into practice and reflecting on whether that practice is as successful as it could have been. What made it work, not work? And taking that learning and applying it in a different context.

That is absolutely my purpose. If they leave with those skills, we've equipped them to deal with an unknowable future. What switched me on to this is a fundamental belief in resilience, which comes from deep learning — which is an uncomfortable process. For me, it's a constructive way of engaging with struggle — in a thoughtful way — and resilience comes from struggle.

Through this you develop confidence — you know that nothing will ever be perfect. It won't turn out as you planned. But, if you approach it with an open mind, there aren't many problems that you can't make some movement on, in a direction you want to go.

Rob: I hear depth of your own philosophy on that, but what about the team you were leading? Was there a shared sense of doing something purposeful together?

Carol: We put a lot of energy into trying to understand and develop: What are the key learnings about this approach that we can make explicit and share with others? How do we know what to take forward into other runs of this programme, to keep the spirit and purpose alive? And, knowing that no two groups of learners and tutors will ever be the same. Therefore, you're looking for alignment, not something standard. But it must be consistent and congruent enough that you don't lose the sense of purpose. You don't want to confuse the cohort of participants by just experimenting.

The five of us in the team from the beginning, went through a learning process together. We went through something called Team Mastery. It was a team coach development programme for us. We also saw the programme being run in other countries. All of those things helped us develop as a team. The process of spending time away together, was important: talking about what to do, how to make it real.

Rob: And having been through that, what do you think they'd say about the purpose of this programme?

Carol: We put time and energy into developing our vision, mission, values and a statement of ethos. We did it together and put it down on paper. It's still evolving now. We had a clear sense of ethos going into the programme. When it came to actually taking up roles as team coaches, I think there was still quite a lot of variation. I think it took around two years, to really work though, and translate into a shared ethos in practice.

The significant bit of learning is: You can write something quite quickly on paper, but how do you interpret, for example, practice-led learning? Put 100 people in a room and they'll all have different ideas of what that means. I'm not sure how feasible it is to have a shared sense of purpose before starting practice, however much theory you've read. At the start, we could trust each other, but our understandings were very different.

Rob: Looking from start of programme to now, how much would you say is a sustainable change that couldn't be reversed?

Carol: I don't think it would be reversed. Part of the university's 2020 strategy is to enhance practice-led learning and teaching. In that context, this is a flagship programme.

I always had a thing about critical mass. What's helped is having the Masters programme rolled out. We've got the sports business and entrepreneurship programme working with Bristol City Community Trust. So, we've extended the programme. There must be 14–15 people involved in delivery and more around the edges — all involved in thinking in these ways.

We've got a learning community, familiar with our methodologies. If 1 person left, the programme wouldn't fall over. It may morph a bit more, but I think it's quite sustainable.

Rob: Knowing what you know about climate, how useful a concept has that been for you in your authority position, to get the programme to where it is now?

Carol: It has been helpful. Especially, the obvious ones around keeping space for idea time and idea support. Because we hadn't done it before, it was really important that other people had their fingerprints all over the programme. It was a collaborative effort to adapt it for our context — transplanting it wouldn't work.

There was me and the delivery team plus a circle of people around the programme, who were influencers and significant stakeholders. One important thing was keeping the buzz in the group around the programme.

Rob: And some of these you had authority over, and some not?

Carol: I didn't have any real formal authority over my team. I don't line manage anybody. I can't tell them to do something if they don't want to do it. That's where I think the climate thing is really important. If you treat people nicely, you have a store of credits. You do need their goodwill. Most people don't want to be obstructive. They end up being obstructive because you dump things on them at short notice. If you've done some seed-sowing and preparing the ground it will mean most people want to help — it's easier for them, as well as you.

Rob: Were there any other bits of the climate concept that were relevant?

Carol: Playfulness was really important because we were doing something quite different and risky. It's nice to have the opportunity to be innovative, but if it falls apart, that's no fun. Creating space and a supportive atmosphere was important. Also, it was really important for the programme that we were seen to be creative. We had to role model an atmosphere and ethos for the programme.

But the thing not in the team climate measure is the extent of support from the wider organisation. To me those key stakeholders were more important than anything else.

Rob: Talking about difference between people — how much was that something you thought about with the team (including the wider team)?

Carol: It was important for us to acknowledge we brought different things to the programme. Different experiences and different ways of thinking about things. This was both helpful and a major source of tension. In the early days, we didn't have a big enough shared core of understanding. One person would go back into teacher mode, as soon as they felt nervous and anxious. What happens is that the team entrepreneurs (TEs) notice and it's inconsistent. But also, you're working hard to get the TEs to work outside their comfort zone. But they go to this person for an 'answer'. And that person is trying to be helpful.

The diversity of thinking styles was helpful, but it's taken time to develop a big enough shared understanding. People will always be different, but there's enough consistency of approach now that it feels solid to both staff and students. Diversity needs a shared sense of why we're doing what we're doing.

Challenge and involvement was the most difficult aspect of climate. We were too high off the scale! It made me sensitive to how you can have too much of something. It took some people so far beyond their comfort zones that it was unhelpful and unproductive.

Rob: If you don't have other aspects of support in there...?

Carol: As an example, in week 3, in our very first year, I was there with another team coach. We went to an area where we had creative conversations around a circular table. One of the new students was busy rearranging all the chairs to point forward. He had marked the two team companies on different sides, with an aisle down the middle, and a podium for the speaker to stand on. He'd felt uncomfortable about having someone, whom he considered an expert, speaking to a circle. He felt the learning should come from the speaker, not from the team.

It was a manifestation of discomfort. The feedback we got was: this isn't what I want. There's an adjustment period. Confidence may take time to build. And being willing to take the risk and say: I do know what I'm doing and it's making a difference. I need to be able to ease these young people into a place of recognising that it's making a difference.

Rob: In retrospect, how much risk taking do you think there has been, from you and wider team?

Carol: I'm not a very good person to ask about that. I felt comfortable that we had senior manager support. I'd flagged up the risks and they had recognised this. I don't believe you can half-do something. The risk is you end up with the worst of both. For instance, we could have stuck our toes in the water and taken students through traditional taught modules with a bit of coaching added to see how it went. But that would have been confusing and inconsistent and I saw that as higher risk than what we were doing.

The other thing about risk is: you want to do the best thing you can. You certainly don't want to do anything that will jeopardise the education of those young people. But, there's always a way back. For risk mitigation I mapped what we were doing in year 1, against the 1st year of our standard degree programmes. For the students who didn't like ours, they could transfer onto a mainstream business and management programme. That was my risk mitigation. If it had all gone wrong, it was a genuine fall-back position.

Rob: Do you remember how many chose to do that?

Carol: I think we had 2 out of 37.

Rob: How far have you and your team used any Creative Problem-Solving tools, for the types of work problems where you needed to come up with ideas?

Carol: Yes, we have and they've been very useful. We have an approach based on the 5 Es, from the Finnish model: aesthetic, education, entertainment, energy and esprit — spirit of the programme. We do brainstorming and we run several innovation challenges each year. Some last a few hours; some last over 48 hours. We have a couple of people in the team who are versed in design thinking. Team entrepreneurs also research their own preferred methods. For instance, a couple of weeks back some of them used our Lego Serious Play kit to explore their leadership.

Rob: What's your experience of how quickly people learn these tools and find them useful?

Carol: I think it varies group to group, and, depending on the problem to be solved. But I think that anything that shakes people up a little, and out of their normal way of thinking, is a good thing. My experience is, a lot of the time, how well it works is down to the group.

I've used Lego with groups, one group loved it; another really struggled to engage with it. I've had groups love 'superheroes'. Ironically older people tend to be more comfortable with it. Maybe 18 year olds are just out of an adolescent stage and 'superheroes' might feel like: 'we're doing kids' stuff'. Whereas in your 30s, it's quite nice to do. My view is you make a wide range of options available and judge the mood, and see what's working, and what else I might try. But, those things have been really important for us as a team.

Case Review

This is an example of a high-profile, radical change in a comparatively risk-averse organisation. There are several points here that make this an interesting case, with some lessons for longer-term sustainability.

First, it's a clear example of the alignment of personal, programme and team purpose, and of the clear thinking that won't allow purpose to be compromised by sectoral and institutional standards. Carol discusses her own focus on learning through 'doing', and how 'doing' with reflection builds confidence and resilience. She describes how, over considerable time, her team evolved a shared understanding of purpose, so that there now exists a critical mass of people who are extending the programme into new realms.

She also describes how she deliberately sought the views of a sceptical, influential individual, so that she thoroughly understood the contextual policies and norms, into which this change would be placed.

The underlying mindset driving this was concerned with ensuring that the programme itself has the desired, positive effect on students. But, to implement such a programme, she had to understand, and demonstrate understanding, of the prevailing cultural systems, procedures and norms. All of these examples have served to grow and maintain clarity of purpose, when challenged in different ways.

Second, the time involved in building and sustaining influence and support is considerable. It is a combination of insurance policy and political leverage. It acts as a 'bank of goodwill'. The perceived radicalness of the change, and its challenge to prevailing ways of working, meant that Carol spent very significant time in building relationships around the university. As she describes, it's the small, unforeseeable problems that 'trip you up'. Support must be in place before these problems emerge, not just at the moment of need. Influence is not transactional — it takes time to build genuine work relationships based on mutual 'give and take'.

Third, Carol's approach to risk taking shows a capacity for differentiation. Not all risks have the same consequences. And mitigation strategies were put in place to provide students with a viable alternative degree route, should they want it. What mattered most was that the purpose was delivered, whereas the process for getting there was less important.

This flexibility of means ensured that her team could experiment with her in delivering the best results. They use creative problem-solving tools partly to aid their creativity, but also, mindfully, to be a role model for the use of tools by the learning students. The philosophical emphasis is on experimentation and learning, and this is aided by a mindset that differentiates between tolerable mistakes that aid learning, and others that affect desired outcomes of the programme.

Fourth, there is a clear focus on creating a healthy climate. In work like this, authority lines are often blurred, and it is debatable to what extent people have power. Compliance is a very blunt tool, when what's needed is the genuine goodwill of the team. There are numerous examples here of deliberately setting out to develop team climate around playfulness, idea time and idea support, while being mindful of when challenge and involvement might be too high.

Fifth, the dynamics of diversity is revealing. In the early stages, when purpose was less clear and less shared, diverse thinking caused problems. There was insufficient common ground to hold the group together, and this created tensions. As purpose become more established, so diversity came to be understood as an asset in the service of purpose.

Last, power is at the heart of the matter. The focus is on learning not teaching. One implication of this is that the coaches' role is to enable learning for the students, through stimulating learners' action and reflection. The coach is not the source of the power, but is more of a conduit, to help the learner understand learning all the better. The appropriate mindset for distributing power is crucial for a full engagement of the learners.

Book Synthesis and Limitations

I want to take a moment to review some of the key themes of this book, because I'm arguing that there is an opportune confluence of trends. I also want to point out the limitations of the book, and the developments that are needed.

First, there is a growing demand for and supply of creativity capabilities which can feed innovation in the workplace. I've presented a synthesis of Rhodes' 1961 framework, adapted to take into account the enabling role of team leadership. Like any exploratory work which crosses boundaries and seeks to integrate research and practice from different fields, this framework needs to be scrutinised and tested further.

Second, our expectations of leaders have changed such that we want them to think carefully about using their power to enable purposeful innovation. In this book, I've touched upon an alternative conception of power — one that is widely used in psychology research, but largely forgotten in the leadership domain. Chapter 2 described the concept of power motivation developed by David McClelland, Abigail Stewart and others. They describe people strong in stage 4 interdependent power, who think about making others feel strong, in the service of a worthwhile cause. In the same chapter, Rob Jackson argues that this mindset of interdependent leadership has been differentiating between superior and average leadership outcomes in recent years.

Leaders do need a way of talking about power. Even with many of the interviews for this book, leaders were uncomfortable in talking about power. They seem ambivalent about power: both wanting it and being ill-at-ease with it. They certainly don't want to talk about it. Too many of us associate power with its venal potential for corruption, exploitation, winning and losing and zero-sum games. This book has tried to suggest a different way of thinking about power — one which gives room to manoeuvre for leaders, by reframing it as a resource to be used, (not ignored), in the service of positive societal change.

My personal experience has been that this model resonates deeply with leaders who realise that, increasingly, they must lead others through influence, rather than direct authority, and seek to sustain the genuine goodwill of their talented team members. However, this stage 4 interdependent model of leadership needs greater coverage and independent evaluation. It is insufficiently described and evaluated in the wider literature. Furthermore, while the leaders described in this book seem to share aspects of the interdependent stage of power, they have not been assessed at any motive level.

Third, leaders are learning to have a key, enabling role in helping others develop creative capabilities and to apply them at work. And their efforts are making a positive difference to people's lives. Giving balanced coverage to these efforts is a worthwhile act. How to continue to do so is a challenge that needs more minds.

Potential Scenarios: Wider Creativity in Society

They were born two years apart, and one can't help but wonder if Frederick W. Taylor and Graham Wallas ever met. Regardless, they'd have recognised the current conversation around the future of work, and the potential for technology to replace jobs. 100 years later, we're discussing many of the same economic and ethical issues, only, this time, the threat to jobs comes from physical and digital machine automation.

Taylor would have approved of the spread of the many practices of efficiency standardised processes, reduced cost and increased quality. He might have been surprised by the bleed of his broad principles into the digital realm, and the rapidly increasing potential for widespread removal of activities within jobs, and even whole jobs. In 2017, Coursera's two most-attended online courses, globally, were 'Machine Learning' and 'Neural Networks and Deep Learning'. Both are designed to deepen skills in the AI realm. The demand is growing for these skills, simultaneously safeguarding jobs for some, while extending the threat to others.

These concerns are real and current. I write this paragraph while travelling by train to work with a UK law firm. Under discussion is the potential for roles within the organisation to be replaced by AI. Part of the discussion will settle on how they might introduce practical creativity to their work, bringing meaningful value to their clients, and safeguarding their roles into the future.

And yet, with a dose of vision and optimism, it's possible to imagine that this could be Wallas' century. He would have been delighted with this emerging interest in creativity, as need for, means of and motivation for creativity converge, resulting in the growing education provision for creativity, innovation and entrepreneurship.

And portraying this tension as either/or a dilemma is not helpful. What's missing in much of the discourse is conversation around how to harness the technological capabilities of AI, and combine this with our moral, ethical and societal wishes for human involvement in work. Technology seems to be way out in front, as one logical step leads to the next. Human voices seem some distance behind.

But it needn't be like this. One of the threads of this book has been that capabilities learnt at work can be brought into other spheres of our lives. A better-educated population, with developed creativity skills, might initiate some interesting changes and even be transformative for society. Imagining into the future, one can see several possible, even concurrent, scenarios for the next 5–10 years.

1. Optimistically: Creative capabilities find their outlet

As more of us become capable in the process of developing novel and useful ideas, so one can imagine flash groups forming at a size to match the scale of the challenge. This might be within and across organisations, at the level of cities, and internationally. Access to digital technology platforms provides the means to bring together networks of people on whatever scale is needed, for as long as the challenge lasts. Since 2010, the social innovation pioneer Open Ideo claims to have brought together hundreds of thousands of people in 202 countries, producing around 16,000 ideas for social good.

It's estimated that by 2050, around two-thirds of the world's population will live in cities. These cities currently occupy less than 5% of the world's landmass but account for around 70% of global energy consumption and greenhouse gas emissions.[3] It takes little to imagine that an increasingly educated workforce will want to contribute to solving the transport, energy, housing, health, education and other problems of the cities in which they will live.

The fundamental idea is that, once we have the capabilities, we can form and reform around challenges that interest us, and scale needn't be an obstacle. This is driven from the ground up. What's less clear is how city politicians and administrators will respond to this rapidly emerging opportunity in their midst.

2. A continued fragmentation

It's also possible to imagine a continuation of what currently prevails. The confluence of personal and organisational need for development of creativity, supported by platforms and suppliers who give access to a wide range of programmes, delivering results that are largely invisible, except within the commercial boundaries of individual organisations.

There is little vision, planning and coordination here, and little by way of positive reinforcement. Efforts are driven largely because of a multitude of individual motives.

One of the potential consequences of such fragmentation and poor value extraction is that we may soon develop a surplus of potential creative capabilities, but with little productive outlet for their use. As Farzad Eskafi, the CEO of Sparcit, pointed out in Chapter 4, divergent thinking capabilities can deteriorate as well as improve. The essence of this scenario is of one step forward, one step back.

3. More far-sighted structural and policy support

The World Economic Forum 2016 report on 'the future of jobs', includes complex problem solving, critical thinking and creativity as three skills which will rise in importance for many sectors. It describes a Fourth Industrial Revolution whereby:

> Developments in genetics, artificial intelligence, robotics, nanotechnology, 3D printing and biotechnology, to name just a few, are all building on and amplifying one another. This will lay the foundation for a revolution more comprehensive and all-encompassing than anything we have ever seen.[4]

And the same report advocates a concerted effort by all stakeholders, in order to adjust to providing the skills needed in the future. This includes reviewing our education provision, starting with school, extending to incentivising lifelong learning, and involving collaboration between governments, business and education and training providers.

This is coordination of creativity learning over time and space. In this scenario, creativity becomes a fundamental component of a society's skill-set, with consensus on its value, and barriers to entry lowered to encourage new skill providers.

Such coordination would be needed across national and local government, educational institutions and workplaces. It would need a genuine, large-scale conversation.

The meaning of work has changed in the last generation. When I started work, in 1987, work was a place. We went to work. Gradually, work became something we did, often disconnected from place. The shift from noun (place) to verb (doing) is significant. We brought work within our scope of choice. We're reaching the point where arguments about learning creativity, innovation and enterprise will soon be redundant because they'll be satisfactorily proven. The big question will be: How do we want to use the human talents we already possess?

References

1. Ardito, M. (1982). *Bell Telephone Magazine*. Creativity: It's the Thought that Counts, Vol. 61 (1). Available at: https://quoteinvestigator.com/2014/03/03/creative-maya/_. (Accessed on 08/03/2018).
2. Collins, B. (2018). The Kings Fund. Available at: https://www.kingsfund.org.uk/publications/innovation-nhs. (Accessed on 22/01/2018).
3. Morphocode. Available at: https://morphocode.com/global-trends-urbanisation/. (Accessed on 21/12/2017).
4. World Economic Forum (2016). Available at: http://reports.weforum.org/future-of-jobs-2016/#xlink. (Accessed on 23/11/2017).

Further Resources

To support your learning, go to the url link below to access creative problem solving tools, other reading and further relevant resources.

To access the supplementary material for further reading, please follow the instructions below:

1. Go to: https://www.worldscientific.com/token/q0185-SUPP.
2. You will next be prompted to register an account/login.
3. Access will be activated upon your account registration/login.
4. Access the supplementary material from: https://www.worldscientific.com/r/boostcreativity-resources.

For subsequent access, simply log in with the same login details in order to access.

For enquiries, please email: sales@wspc.com.sg.

Index

A
ABCD framework, 173
ABCD model, 46, 61
abuses of power, 29
Accenture, 12, 103
accountability, 42
achievement motive, 32, 37, 57
adaptability, 168
adaption-innovation, 134
adaption-innovation and work attraction, 147
adaption-innovation theory, 142, 147
adaptive preference, 135
adaptive style, 135
affiliation motive, 32, 36
agile, 67
A-I theory, 139, 153, 162
Akatemia, 176
alignment, 50
alignment of personal, programme and team purpose, 183
Amabile, Teresa, 107
ambiguity, 17
ambulance service, 91
Anderson, Neil, 52
anxiety, 16, 63, 90, 101
anxiety levels, 18
apply affirmative judgement, 75
Aravind Eye Care, 53
aroused motivation, 109
assertive, 34
Atherton, Phil, 114
Atkinson, John, 31
attainability, 53
authority, 6, 27
awareness of impact on others, 169

B
benchmark, 128
benefits to broader society, 10
Besemer, 51
black box, 15
black sheep of innovation, 6
Blakeley, Karen, 30
bounded experimentation, 129
Boyatzis, Richard, 16, 151
brainstorming, 84, 91, 94
brainwriting, 84
breakthrough thinking, 148
bridger, 141, 169

Bridging, 153
Broadway, Alice, 97
Buffalo State College, 66
buffer, 90
Burnham, David, 36
Buttner, Holly, 142
buy-in, 126
Byrne, Cristina, 106

C

capacity for creativity and innovation, 5
challenge and involvement, 110, 181
check your objectives, 76
chief innovation officers, 13
chronic stress, 16
Cicero, 29
cities, 187
clarity, 52
Claxton, Guy, 106
client, 77
climate, 106, 180
climate and team performance, 128
climate for innovation, 105
climate impact on performance, 109
climate is a 'lead' indicator, 128
climate measurement, 117
climate research, 109
clinical evidence, 121
coaching, 27, 125, 127
cognitive gap, 138, 149
cognitive structure, 135
collaboration, 13, 22
Collins, Jim, 41
communities and cities, 22
complexity of feelings, 101
complex trends, 17
conflict, 112
constructing opportunities, 78

consumers, 8, 49
control and predictability, 20
convergent phase, 84
convergent thinking, 68, 77, 88
convergent thinking, principles, 75
coping, 149
coping behaviour, 139
coping strategies, 149
coursera, 11, 186
creating a healthy climate, 128
creative and critical thinking, 11
Creative Education Foundation, 66
creative life, 9
creative person, 7
creative press, 7
creative problem solving, 47, 67, 123, 182
Creative Problem-Solving, description, 67
creative problem-solving model, 77
creative problem-solving tools, 61
creative process, 7, 65
creative product, 7
creative-writing workshop, 96
creativity, 4, 120
creativity and purposeful outcomes, 51
creativity definition, 6
creativity training, 72
crisis of trust, 29
criteria, 81
critical mass, 180
criticisms of creativity research, 52
customers, 13
cynicism and suspicion, 21

D

debate, 113
Decide Madrid, 12

defer judgement, 72
degree of change, 51
Deloitte, 9
democratised, 9
dependence, 33
designers, 142
design for incubation time, 89
design iterations, 88
develop ideas, 5
diabetes risk line, 127
diabetes services, 125
diagnostic and navigation skills, 89
digital initiatives, 8
discretionary effort, 110
divergent thinking, 65, 68, 77, 149
divergent thinking, principles, 72
divergent thinking skills, 69
diverse teams, 139
diverse thinking, 184
diversity, 18, 101, 170
diversity of thinking styles, 181
drug and alcohol dependency team, 93

E
Ekvall, Goran, 110, 113
elaboration, 69
emergent, 17
emotion, 44
emotional intelligence, 100
emotional states, 152
empathy, 168
employability, 6
engineering students, 143
enterprise, 11
entrepreneurs, 142
Eskafi, Farzad, 69
evaluating options, 68

evaluation, 106
everyday innovation, 55–56
executives, 71
existing structure, 136
experiment, 184
experimentation and learning, 184
exploring data, 79
extensions, 104
EY, 8, 57

F
facilitate the team, 90
facilitator, 77, 83
FleishmanHillard, 49
flexibility, 69, 100, 184
fluency, 69, 100
focusing stage, 95
Forbes, 14
force-fitting, 97
Ford, Martin, 10
frame the conversation around a common goal, 153
framing problems, 79–80
freedom, 111
frontline, 56

G
game changers, 104
generate novelty, 83
generating ideas, 82
glimpses of the new, 15
go for quantity, 72
Goleman, Daniel, 16
goodwill, 110, 174, 180, 185
grounds for optimism, 22
Gryskiewicz, Nur, 142
Gryskiewicz, Stanley, 84
Guilford, Joy Paul, 69

H

habitual thinking, 17
happiness, 107
Harris, Robert, 29
Harris, Shelley, 96
having impact, 33
healthy climate, 184
higher purpose, 30
human-centred design thinking, 67
humility, 42
humour and playfulness, 107
humour and spontaneity, 112

I

Idea Economy, 12
idea elaboration, 100
idea implementation, 29
idea support, 112
idea time, 111
ideation platforms, 13
illumination, 21, 64
imagination, 79
impact, 36
implementation, 7, 177–178
implementation testing, 29
implicit motives, 43
improved divergent thinking, 71
incremental, 21
incremental improvement, 72
incrementalism, 104
incremental performance, 13
incubation, 21, 64
independence, 34
influence, 36, 44, 79
inhibition, 36
innovation, 4, 7, 103
innovation and reification, 14
innovation bind, 15
innovation catalysts, 22
innovation definition, 6
innovation performance, 13
innovative style, 136
Institutional Leader, 35, 37–38
interdependent, 35
interdependent expression of power, 54
interdependent leader, 41, 57
interdependent-minded leader, 100, 129
interdependent model of leadership, 186
interdependent power, 39–40
interest, 78
interviews, 5
Isaksen, Scott, 78, 106

J

Jackson, Rob, 41, 185
Jaimovich, Nir, 10
Jarvis, Carol, 56, 175
job satisfaction, 157
Jyväskylä University of Applied Sciences, 174

K

KAI preference, 137, 143
KAI score, 141, 144, 157
Kaizen improvement, 148
Keats, John, 63
keep novelty alive, 76
Kirton, Michael, 134
Kirton's Adaption-innovation Inventory (KAI), 136
Koestler, Arthur, 103
Kurtzberg, Terri, 139

L

leader and the problem-solving process, 141
leaders enabling innovation, 44
leadership, 4, 11
leadership and power, 30
leadership development, 28
leadership impact on climate, 109
leading others, 11
leading teams for better problem solving, 152
lead others through influence, 185
lean, 67
lean approaches, 148
learning, 154, 173, 180, 183
learning and development functions, 9
learning creativity, innovation and enterprise, 189
learning in divergent thinking, 72
learning leaders, 4
Lego, 183
level, 135
level of influence, 178
LIFT, 91
Lithium Technologies, 8
Litwin, George, 32
local leadership, 108
loose focusing, 85
Lotus Blossom, 96

M

Machine Learning, 186
MacKinnon, Donald, 51
Maier, Norman, 80
make connections, 73
managing cognitive diversity, 139
marginal gains, 148
match styles to different phases of work, 154
match styles to work demands, 154
McClelland, David, 30, 36, 185
McKinsey, 8
metacognition, 22
middle managers, 56
millennials, 10
mindset, 118, 183
mindset for distributing power, 184
MIT's Senseable City Laboratory, 81
mixed feelings, 129
Moore, Karl, 9, 57
Morgan, Henry, 31
morphological analysis, 84
motivation, 149, 170
motive, 32, 134, 139
multiplier effect, 22
Murray, Christiana, 31
mutuality, 40, 129

N

National Science Foundation, 70
nature of work, 28
need to be liked, 36
negative capability, 63
Neural Networks and Deep Learning, 186
new-in-context, 7
new technologies, 10
Noller, Ruth, 67
non-routine roles, 10
normal distribution, 137
Northumbria University, 175
novelty, 16, 51

O

omni-disciplinary approaches, 101
Open Ideo, 187
opportunity, 134
originality, 69, 100
Osborn, Alex, 65
outsourcing, 10

P

paired comparison analysis, 88
pairing with each other, 154
paradox, 44
paradox and complexity, 40
paradox of structure, 138
Parnes, Sidney, 66, 83
patient flow, 160
patterns of repetition, 15
Pauling, Linus, 73
people, 46
perseverance, 90
personal goals, 36
personal identification with organisations, 49
personal power, 34, 41
personal power leaders, 37
pioneers of learning, 22
playfulness, 181
polarise decisions, 45
political and social process, 28
poor team climates, 109
power, 6, 29–30, 184–185
power and politics, 29
power misuse, 30
power motive, 33, 36, 54
power motive and leadership, 33
power motive training, 40
practical implications for leaders, 89
practice-based learning, 56
preparation, 21, 64
preparing for implementation, 87
press, 46, 105
pressure hangover, 108
pressure valve on change, 129
Previde, Guido, 143
principle of extended effort, 83
Problem A, 140
Problem B, 140
problem minded, 89
problem statements, 80
process, 46
process-based view of creativity, 65
product, 46
prototypes, 88
psychological holding mechanisms, 15
psychological safety, 17, 19, 100, 107
Puccio, Gerard, 106
purpose, 30, 179, 184
purpose — crafting, 55
purpose-driven companies, 50
purposeful goal, 170
purposeful work, 10

Q

quality of human interaction, 11

R

radical, 21
radical change, 13, 72, 183
radical innovations, 52
random object tool, 74
random word, 99
Ratti, Carlo, 55, 81
rehabilitation of power, 36
reification, 14
renovate, 104
research and practice, 47
resource group, 77
returning authority to others, 41

reversal, 91
Rhodes, Mel, 7, 45, 51, 173, 185
Rieple, Alison, 142
risk-averse, 105
risk taking, 17, 113, 122, 182
role attractiveness, 143
Rotondi, 143
routine roles, 10

S

sandwich generation, 6
say why, 154
scientific management, 20
screening, 68
search for ideas, 8
search for purpose, 54
seek novelty, 73
self-actualisation, 11
self-awareness, 169
self-management, 168
sharedness, 53
shortlisted ideas, 83
shortlisting, 68
Siebrecht, Adrienne, 32
Simpson, Peter, 63
Situational Outlook Questionnaire (SOQ), 114, 119, 123
Siu, Henry, 10
skills of creativity, 22
social-emotional maturity, 33
social good, 4
socialised goals, 36
social payoff, 90
Solverboard, 114
sorting, 68
South West Leadership Academy, 54, 91
Sparcit, 69
spontaneity, 107
spread of ideas, 7

stage-gate innovation process, 104
stay focused, 76
Stewart, Abigail, 33, 185
strategic vision, 121
strategy, 13
stress, 157
Stringer, 109
strong adaptor, 163
style, 51, 135

T

Taylor, Frederick, 20, 186
team climate, 36, 47, 108
team climate diagnostic, 53
Team Entrepreneurship programme, 175–176
teams, 5
The more adaptive, 145–146
The more innovative, 145–146
threat, 106
time for developing and implementing ideas, 120
time pressure, 108
tipping point, 169
Torrance, Paul, 69
Torrance tests of creative thinking, 69
Totterdell, Peter, 51
TRIZ, 67
trust, 4, 17, 19, 100, 107
trust and openness, 111
Tullett, Arthur, 143
tunnel-visioned, 106

U

UK health sector, 174
uncertainty, 17
uncertainty and ambiguity, 63, 101
unconscious, 43, 65
understanding the challenge, 78

University of the West of England (UWE), 174–175
unpredictability, 28
UWE Business School, 91

V
value, 7
Venkataswamy, Govindappa, 53
verification, 21, 64, 87
vision, 53
visionary nature, 52
VW, 29

W
Wallas, Graham, 21, 63, 186–187
Wazoku, 13, 55
wealth-creating ideas, 12

Webb Young, James, 65
Weinberger, Mark, 57
well-defined problem statement, 80
West, Michael, 52
Whitman, Meg, 12
wicked problems, 174
Widdows, Charlie, 114
work design, 106
work focus, 40
workload, 17
work productivity, 157
work purpose, 129

Y
Yilmaz, Seda, 143